FABRIC
JOURNEY

An Inside Look at the Quilts of
Ruth B. McDowell

C&T PUBLISHING

Text and Artwork © 2005 Ruth B. McDowell
Publisher: Amy Marson
Editorial Director: Gailen Runge
Acquisitions Editor: Jan Grigsby
Editor: Lynn Koolish
Technical Editor: Joyce Lytle
Copyeditor/Proofreader: Darra Williamson/Wordfirm Inc.
Cover Designer: Christina D. Jarumay
Design Director/Book Designer: Christina D. Jarumay
Production Assistant: Tim Manibusan
Photographyt: David Caras except as noted
Published by C&T Publishing, Inc., P.O. Box 1456, Lafayette, California
94549

Front cover: *Oseberg Ship*, © 2003 Ruth B. McDowell
Back cover: *A Rash of Flamingoes, Ikat Anemones, and Reflections*

Attention Teachers: C&T Publishing, Inc., encourages you to use this
book as a text for teaching. Contact us at 800-284-1114 or
www.ctpub.com for more information about the C&T Teachers Program.

We take great care to ensure that the information included in this book
is accurate and presented in good faith, but no warranty is provided
nor results guaranteed. Having no control over the choices of materials
or procedures used, neither the author nor C&T Publishing, Inc., shall
have any liability to any person or entity with respect to any loss or
damage caused directly or indirectly by the information contained in
this book. For your convenience, we post an up-to-date listing of correc-
tions on our web page (www.ctpub.com). If a correction is not already
noted, please contact our customer service department at
ctinfo@ctpub.com or at P.O. Box 1456, Lafayette, CA 94549.

Trademarked (™) and Registered Trademark (®) names are used
throughout this book. Rather than use the symbols with every occur-
rence of a trademark or registered trademark name, we are using the
names only in the editorial fashion and to the benefit of the owner,
with no intention of infringement.

Library of Congress Cataloging-in-Publication Data
McDowell, Ruth B.
  A fabric journey an inside look at the quilts of ruth b. mcdowell / Ruth
B. McDowell.
      p. cm.
  Includes bibliographical references and index.
  ISBN 1-57120-279-X
  1. Quilting–Patterns. 2. Patchwork–Patterns. I. Title.

TT835.M244 2005
746.46'041–dc22

                    2004015852

Printed in China
10 9 8 7 6 5 4 3 2 1

DEDICATION

To my daughters, Emily and Leah, who've been part of this journey from the beginning.

ACKNOWLEDGMENTS

I would like to thank my good friends and fellow quilt-makers Nancy Halpern, Rhoda Cohen, and Sylvia Einstein for sharing their eyes and hearts and wisdom over 25 years. I couldn't have done this without them.

I would also like to extend my gratitude to Pfaff for their support and for their wonderful sewing machines. The integrated dual-feed makes the piecing go much more easily. It is also a pleasure to use Hobbs batting, a really quality product.

To all of my students, I owe a real debt for asking the good questions—questions that open the discussion and push the learning process for all of us.

CONT

Introduction

I like quilts that you can look at for a long time. The seeds for my quilts spring from things that absolutely amaze me in themselves: a tree or a place, a group of people or a plant, a ship or a stone. My quilts are an attempt to record and celebrate the unique characteristics of these subjects, and my responses to them.

THE PIECING PROCESS...

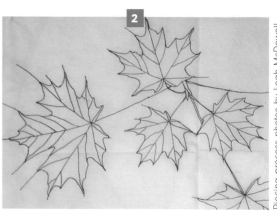

Piecing process photos by Leah McDowell

The Quilt Designs

I usually select either an impressionistic interpretation of a natural subject or an object from the human world as the starting point for a particular quilt. At the same time, each quilt is a conscious exploration of the pieced-quilt medium, and a collage of fabrics old and new. As I work on the quilt, it assumes many more meanings than the relatively simple idea from which it began. In many ways, it would be easier simply to create an abstract design, without attempting to base the design on a particular topic.

My quilts are visual compositions in line, color, and pattern, as well as interpretations of the inspirational subject; they must work graphically from a distance as well as reward close study of the details. The use of commercial fabrics contributes to this outcome, not only with their variety of colors and patterns, but also because of the historical and emotional connections these fabrics make.

Fabrics have been part of the human experience, providing comfort and warmth for thousands of years. Technically, it would often be much easier to dye or paint the fabrics I need, but the deliberate use of the same fabrics found in clothing and furnishing in my quilts links both the quiltmaker (me) and the viewer to other lives and times, whether or not we are intellectually aware of that connection.

THE PIECING PROCESS

At the center of my quiltmaking is the fact that my quilts are assembled in a traditional machine-pieced, right-sides-together format. Artwork exists as the result of a process; that is, the artist working, over a period of time, in whatever medium he or she selects, to express something that did not exist before. Understanding and working with (and sometimes against) the chosen medium is the craft of the artist. The *how* is an intimate part of the work. The seamlines in my quilts are both lines in the depiction of the image *and* structural components of the process.

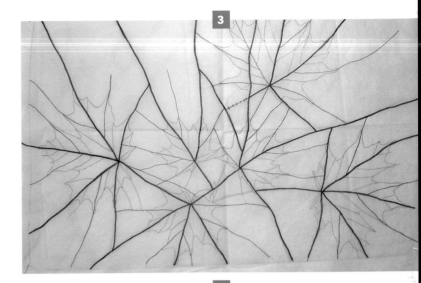

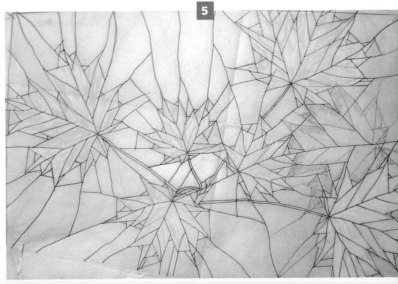

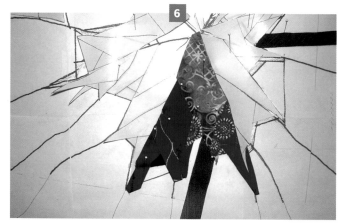

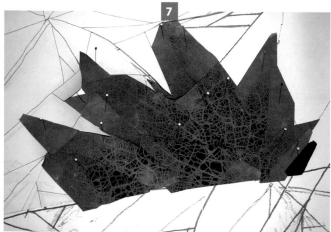

The piecing process I use is a complicated one, but one that I enjoy tremendously. Planning the structure in detail before I begin sewing gives me a chance to relate the physical seaming to the artistic expression. How I will put the pieces together is very closely tied to the original inspiration for the quilt design.

This begins to sound like a fairly far-fetched "religion." I believe, however, that the structure of the piecing process gives integrity to the surface with an underlying connectedness that may not be apparent at first glance. In this way, my quilts are much different in construction, in concept, and—to the perceptive viewer—in result, than appliquéd or fused art quilts.

One of the great advantages of piecing a quilt as I do is that a pieced background made from a variety of fabrics provides a richer surface than a single background fabric. By deliberately designing a pieced background that is an integral element of the quilt, the construction of the quilt, which I consider a significant part of the design, is more clearly shown.

ARTISTIC EXPRESSION

The shape and scale of the individual pieces, the design of the major and minor seamlines—in fact, the entire engineering of a pieced quilt—can be a source of artistic expression that underlies the fabrics and colors of the surface. The limits inherent in simple piecing force simplification and a certain degree of abstraction. Whether or not the casual viewer perceives this, the process gives a depth and strength to my work that is not present in most other ways of working with fabric.

My quilts are quite unabashedly *quilts*. They do not pretend to be paintings. Their construction, pieced right-sides-together in the old traditional way, and the eclectic mix of commercial fabrics I use to make them, both contribute to this quality.

The Fabrics

In planning a quilt, I first make a piecing drawing—black lines on white paper. Each line will become a seamline between two pieces of fabric. I don't color the drawing before I begin, preferring to color with the actual fabric pieces cut to the size they will be in the quilt. Small-scale maquettes (or mock-ups) are not particularly useful to me in planning my work. For one thing, colors work differently at a small scale than they do in a full-size quilt. More importantly, I find that the variety of patterned fabrics I use and the importance of these prints in the overall composition make it necessary for me to work full size.

CHOOSING AND USING FABRIC

When I collect fabrics for my quilts, and then choose which fabric to use for each piece of the design, the pattern (or print) on the fabric becomes almost as important as the color. This is a difficult concept to explain unless you have tried to work with such a wide range of fabrics yourself. In my weeklong classes, after each student creates her design, she begins to choose fabrics. As she pins potential pieces of fabric to her drawing to audition them, she begins to develop a sense for the process.

Choosing the right fabric is not a process that can be expressed verbally or reduced to a formula, but rather an intensely visual process. In making the selection for a single piece, the quiltmaker may pin a series of nearly identical fabrics on her design, step back to view the result, take that fabric down, and try yet another. Eventually she will arrive at the fabric that fits, and it is fascinating to me how often everyone else in the class agrees *immediately*, based on a purely visual response. To explain what happened *in words* is quite another issue. Sometimes it's a matter of the fabric being just the right value. Sometimes it's the right scale or mix of colors in the fabric print, or the substitution of a plaid or geometric pattern for a swirling motif. The potential pool of fabric choices contributes to the process.

VISUAL IMPACT

The right fabric is always chosen in the context of the design. Quilt teacher and designer Lorraine Torrence tells her students: "Make visual decisions visually." This is wise advice. You must keep your eyes open and be aware of what is taking place in the developing quilt. Don't let intellectual explanations of fabric choices override the visual impact of your selections.

For instance, some students have been handed such formulas as "Red advances, and blue recedes." My response to this is: "Well, *sometimes*." In standard

color-class exercises, with painted samples, that may appear to be the case. But depending on the context—that is, the composition of the design, the colors, patterns, and placement and proportion of the fabrics assembled—the opposite may be true *and* the effect can be achieved.

I encourage my students to be open to the visual impact each fabric makes and to depend on that reaction rather than to rely on a formula or a verbal theory. The late beloved quilt instructor Doreen Speckmann described the auditioning process as follows: "Put a fabric up on the design wall. Are you happy it arrived? Take it away. Do you miss it?" (For more about Doreen, see pages 14–17.)

BUILDING A FABRIC STASH

It is crucial to have access to a wide range of different types and scales and kinds of patterned fabric. If you don't have it, you can't learn to use it. You *must* have a stash of fabric to work from. I've built up quite an eclectic collection over the years: mostly cottons with a few linens and silks. These fabrics come from different eras, sources, and parts of the world. Because I prefer to have many choices and have limited space to store them, the fabric pieces themselves are usually less than a yard in length.

UNUSUAL FABRICS

Many students are intrigued, but mystified, by the many unusual (to the traditional quilt world) patterns in the fabrics I use in my quilts. They often like the quilts, but don't comprehend the fabric selection process.

Lately some students have been bringing really wild fabrics to class, apparently thinking I can wave my magic hands and make these fabrics into great quilts. There is a little more discrimination involved in fabric selection than that.

It is crucial that you remain visually aware of the overall composition of the quilt when making the fabric choices. You must move around the room (or use a reducing glass or some similar device) to view the quilt from varying distances and perspectives. This enables you to determine how the fabrics interact both up close and from a distance, to remain aware of the focus of the quilt, and to monitor the balance of the composition as a whole.

You must also be visually honest with yourself about what is happening with the quilt composition as you choose the fabrics you will use to make it. The quilt should make the complete statement; it should not need any printed text or verbal explanation to convey your message. If the statement is not clear visually, the quilt is not a successful piece.

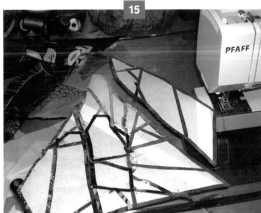

These fabric pieces are a finite resource. I often can't find more of a specific fabric if I run out of it—nor would I want to. To my mind, this is a challenge rather than a disaster, and the solution usually produces a more interesting quilt. It forces me to change direction and solve the problem by introducing alternate fabrics. This appears to make the whole process more difficult at the time since it requires making even more decisions. But finding the ideal alternative fabric ultimately makes the design richer, and much more interesting, than if I had enough of what I thought I needed in the first place.

FABRIC MAKES THE QUILT

Every new quilt presents an opportunity to use fabric in a way that perfectly supports the intent of the quilt. Each quilt presented in this book includes a discussion of why the fabrics were selected so you can begin to understand my thought process when selecting fabric.

The Borders

The design composition of a pieced quilt may include border elements. Sometimes a border works like a frame on a painting, setting off the central area of the quilt. Some quilts benefit from a disrupted border that disappears and reappears around the quilt's perimeter, while some do best with a border on just one or two sides to balance the compositional elements of the design. Other compositions don't need borders at all.

I don't want a border that traps my quilt in a tight box. The design must be accessible and it must be able to breathe. Planning a border is specific to each individual quilt; there are no specific "rules." Throughout this book, you will see many different border decisions with each discussed in the text that accompanies the quilt.

The Quilting

I do all of my own quilting on my home sewing machines, usually by dropping the feed dogs, switching to a darning foot, and then free-motion stitching. I treat the quilting as a chance to sketch a linear pattern on the pieced surface in a way that enhances the design as well as holds the layers together.

I often do this stitching without marking any lines on the quilt, preferring a looser approach much like sketching with a pencil. This is easier said than done, and is a place I'd like to get to rather than a spot I feel I've arrived at! Quilting on a sewing machine is technically difficult, and a process that generally allows one chance to do well. It is very hard, sometimes impossible, to remove machine-quilted stitches and try again. There is a quickness to pencil sketching that allows for gestural lines that can be difficult to achieve in the cramped and laborious business of machine (or sometimes even hand) quilting.

As with every other element of my quilts, the quilting is unique and specific to each quilt. You can read about the quilting choices for each quilt presented.

This Is a Visual Process

As a teacher, I encourage students to design their own pieced quilts and to eventually develop a style of working with the fabric that is both personal and unique. As an artist, I find great excitement in making my own quilts and exploring how to adapt the seaming and fabrics to express what I see. When I am working in my studio, the entire process is intensely visual, with decisions made because of what the various options looked like, what seemed interesting, what fabrics I had, and so on.

When I'm teaching, students want some verbal explanation of that visual process. They want me to explain in words what I see and think as I am working on my art quilts. As a result, I have been trying for years to tease into words a description of a process that is inherently non-verbal.

This book is an attempt to do just that, using eighteen of my recent quilts as the basis for discussion and example. I've tried to reconstruct some of the visual process I experienced as I created each quilt in a way that may be helpful to other quiltmakers or students of art quilts.

 FREE-MOTION QUILTING

After years of quilting, I've come up with a process that works for me. You can follow these few suggestions for free-motion quilting and see if they work for you:

1. Use a slightly heavier backing fabric than you would normally choose for hand quilting. The sewing machine doesn't care about the weight of the fabric, and a slightly heavier back will not shift, pleat, or warp as easily as a lighter-weight piece. I usually use a drapery chintz or twill that I have washed first to preshrink it.

2. Use a cotton batting. The layers adhere better with a cotton batting than with a polyester batting. I use an unbleached organic batting from Hobbs.

3. Pin the layers together rather than thread-basting them. Because I hate to fasten safety pins, I use IBC glass-headed silk pins, 1³/₈" long. I take two stitches on each pin—in and out, in and out—which doubles the friction and buries more of the pin. (I once considered making a breastplate and gauntlets to wear when I work with straight pins, but never got around to it. Actually, I find I don't get scratched very often if I'm careful.) On the other hand, use safety pins if it will likely be months before you finish the quilting.

4. Don't remove any pins until you are about to sew over them. Now you will find the straight pins easier to remove than safety pins.

5. Don't bother to roll up the excess quilt carefully to fit under the arm of the sewing machine; just shove it under there. Then write a letter to your sewing-machine manufacturer requesting an increase in the space under the arm.

6. The outside edge of the quilt takes most of the wear and tear while you are quilting. With a great deal of practice and lots of care, and by following all of the suggestions above, I find I can quilt the outside 12" or so first, then move inward toward the center.

Keep in mind—this works for me— it may not work for you!

Keep in mind that this process relies on:

> How I feel about the subject of the quilt,
> How the drawing is turning out,
> What fabric I have,
> How the fabrics talk to each other,
> The time of year I'm working on the quilt,
> What the weather's been like lately,
> What I've seen recently,
> What I remember having seen,
> What's going on in the world,
> What the last quilt looked like...
> And probably a lot of other stuff as well.

All of this comes from my own thought process and my experience over 30 years of making quilts. It *is not* the result of a course of academic study, nor is it influenced by reading books or taking workshops. It *is* influenced strongly by investing a tremendous amount of time and attention to both the teaching process and to the making of my quilts. The interaction with students is one of the most rewarding parts of my career.

But, in the end, I am just telling you what I think and feel. I could be wrong. You may have other ideas.

I hope those of you who are quiltmakers will find the quilts and the text interesting, informative, and inspirational to developing your own designs. For those of you who don't make quilts (at least not yet), I hope you will enjoy the quilts and come to understand a little more about the process.

Enjoy the show.

These quilts are one-of-a-kind artworks. The designs may not be copied or reproduced in any form without permission. There are no patterns available.

Leaves of Another Year, 50" x 34", © 2003 Ruth B. McDowell

SLIDING GODDESS WITH HEART

Sliding Goddess with Heart, 34" x 49", © 1998 Ruth B. McDowell

The quilt world is a colorful place, full of the most colorful people. The late Doreen Speckmann, a fellow teacher and a quiltmaker from Madison, Wisconsin, was truly unique. A very large woman with a wonderful sense of humor, Doreen often broke up the intense atmosphere at workshops by getting us up and dancing the Electric Slide. She was a very intelligent, very observant (her peripheral vision was amazing!), very warm, and very, *very* funny woman.

A number of years ago, I came across a snapshot taken by Margaret Peters, another fellow teacher. The photo was taken in the auditorium at Asilomar, a conference center in California where we often taught, and Doreen is leading the Electric Slide. At the time, Doreen was going through a tough patch in her life, and I decided on the spot to make her a portrait quilt.

The Quilt Design

I began the drawing with Doreen. As I developed the piecing of Doreen's dancing figure, I extended some construction seams from her figure across the background of the quilt to divide the quilt into sewable sections. By planning the major construction seams in this way, I drew the focus to Doreen and carried the motion of her dance across the whole surface of the quilt. While I intended to machine piece most of the quilt, I decided to hand appliqué Doreen's profile to get that little seam exactly right.

KEEPING THE FOCUS ON DOREEN

After drawing Doreen, I drew in the four-and-a-half student dancers who form the supporting cast. I fractured their shapes slightly with the construction seams coming from Doreen, and included less detail in their figures than I had for Doreen. This simplified them while still giving them character and movement.

Above the dancers, and again deliberately broken by the construction seams, I blocked out the areas for five quilts, angling them as though they were hanging from the ceiling and dancing as well. I drew construction seams in the floor area as gentle arcs to follow the swinging motions of the dance.

The Fabric

I began making the fabric choices for Doreen as well. I found an area on a tan batik with a darker area that suggested an eye. I love the implied face created by this piece of fabric—much better than a literally drawn face. I chose fabrics for Doreen's jacket, shirt, skirt, and

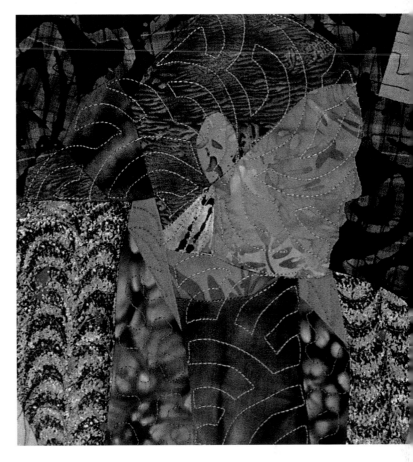

hair ribbon that suggested her style of clothing. Of course, she also had to be wearing Birkenstocks and her signature gold bracelet.

DRESSING THE DANCERS

The clothing fabrics for the other dancers were chosen to work with the fabrics I had selected for Doreen. Quilters tend to favor denim, so I dressed them in jeans in a variety of blues to go with the blues in Doreen's clothing. I found a piece of flowered white shirt to cut up for their sneakers: the flowers resembled shoe laces.

WOODEN FLOOR FABRICS

Merrill Hall, the auditorium at Asilomar, has a wooden floor. I found a printed plaid just slightly lighter on the back than on the front to use for the floor, and used it both right and wrong side up to give it some variety. I tipped the pieces at different angles so the floor would appear to be dancing too.

PUMPKINS

Pumpkins, 57" x 44½", © 1998 Ruth B. McDowell

One spring I scratched some holes and planted a few pumpkin seeds among the Norway maple stumps beside the driveway in my suburban front yard. Didn't cultivate, didn't fertilize, didn't water all summer. The results: huge green leaves, bright yellow flowers, and—in the fall—twelve smooth, big, round, heavy, gloriously orange pumpkins. What magic!

Those pumpkins became the excuse to begin this quilt. As the process got under way, the composition of the quilt was determined as much by the collection of fabrics I had on hand, and the relation of the piecing process to the design, as it was to the pumpkins.

The Quilt Design

In making the drawing for *Pumpkins*, I placed three round pumpkins with curved seams in the lower left corner of the composition. I balanced the pumpkins with several large leaves to the right that I drew with both angled and straight seams. I extended some of the straight seams for ease of piecing, to divide the quilt into sections for sewing, and to visually fracture the background. The straight and angled seams in the leaves contrast with and emphasize the roundness of the pumpkins.

After drawing the pumpkins and leaves, and extending some straight seams as construction lines, I considered the overall composition of the drawing before planning the border.

The Fabric

The only color decision I made when beginning *Pumpkins* was that the pumpkins would be orange. I had planned the seaming of the quilt in such a way that I could sew most of the pumpkin pieces together before adding background fabrics, so I began by selecting fabrics for the pumpkins and cutting those fabric pieces.

CARRYING THE COLOR ACROSS THE QUILT

The orange pumpkins pinned to the lower left corner of my piecing diagram suggested the need to use orange fabrics elsewhere in the quilt for balance. Rather than running out to the fabric shop, I turned—as usual—to my fabric collection, where I found a Hoffman batik with dabs of orange on a pink, green, and gray background.

Since the batik had hints of green and pink in it, I investigated the pink section of my stash. I found a raspberry-pink and lime-green fabric, hand-dyed by Judy Robertson—a fabric that delighted me when I bought it, but it had been waiting for the right quilt to call it home. I had a whole yard of this fabric, and when I put the pink and green hand-dye next to the orange pumpkins and the batik, it looked terrific.

As is often the case, working with the actual fabrics, rather than from a carefully painted maquette, allowed

THOUGHTS ON FABRIC SHOPPING

When I am shopping and see a fabric that intrigues me, I often purchase a fat quarter or a half-yard piece. I usually have no idea how I will use it, and it may mellow on the shelf for five or ten years before it finds its way into a quilt. The batik with the orange dabs—one of the stranger batiks Hoffman has made—and the pink and green hand-dye are good examples.

It's intriguing to consider how the development of the quilt image relates to the fabrics I happen to have on hand. In another year, working from the same drawing, I would have made a very different pumpkin quilt.

my eyes to suggest combinations that my brain might not have made. I don't think I would have envisioned bright pink and chartreuse next to the pumpkins if the fabrics hadn't led me in that direction.

FABRICS FOR LEAVES

I chose a number of greens for the pumpkin leaves, including some lighter and some darker yellowish or bluish greens. The limey greens in the leaves related to the chartreuse in the pink and green hand-dye. One of the darker greens was a vintage fabric—probably from

the 1950s—that my friend Rhoda Cohen found some-where in Maine. It had a printed pattern of shadowed buttons in pink, white, and light brown. The pink related to the other pinks in the quilt and the white buttons lent a sparkle to the surface of the leaves. I used the button fabric in the quilt because I liked it there. If it bothers you that there are buttons on the pumpkin leaves, you can think of them as dewdrops or insect damage.

The Border

The border on a quilt functions much like the frame on a painting. Some quilts do not need borders, just as some paintings do not need significant frames. Sometimes, however, a frame visually sets off a painting and the same holds true for many quilts. In this case, I felt the composition of the quilt needed a border detail—specifically, a few seams parallel to the edges of the quilt. I also felt the additional seams would add more interest to the upper left area of the composition.

I built the border within the edges of the quilt drawing, fracturing it with the proposed seamlines. I also inter-rupted the border with the pumpkins and the leaves. The resulting border frames the piece, respecting the rectangle formed by the edges of the quilt, and enhancing (but not confining) the image the way many traditional quilt borders do.

The Quilting

I free-motion quilted *Pumpkins* with variegated cotton threads. I used a green thread to draw quilted veins on the leaves and variegated orange threads to quilt the pumpkins. An allover fan quilting pattern, reminiscent of a traditional hand quilting design, was used to tie the background together.

To my eye, the overall pattern retreated into the surface and united the background fabrics. This type of quilting is not as visible or noticeable as, for example, the care-fully drawn veins in the pumpkin leaves. The overall pattern also flattened the background, emphasizing the low relief of the pumpkins and leaves.

THOUGHTS ON FINDING THE RIGHT FABRIC

I like areas of bright white in a quilt like this to keep the design from becoming too dense and to add a feeling of airiness; in fact, I make an effort to search out fabrics with a fair amount of bright white. In this quilt, I used several of these fabrics: a tie-dye, a print, a hand-printed piece, an Indian print with small orange flowers (miniature pumpkins, now that I think about it), and a pink and green flowery vintage print with a white background.

One reason to accumulate a stash is to acquire fabrics from other eras. These fabrics use different colors and combinations of colors than you will find in contemporary fabrics, as well as different types and scales of pattern. By including this vari-ety of fabrics, rather than just hand-dyes or con-temporary batiks, you'll give your quilt a much richer surface.

MILKWEED PODS

T his tall, widespread plant has dusky pink flowers beloved by butterflies. In the autumn, the flowers are followed by fat, pointed pods. As the pods mature, they split open to reveal flat brown seeds arranged in an overlapping pattern similar to fish scales.

White silken fibers attached to each seed are packed tightly in the center of the pod. As the weather gets colder, the pods open wider and release the silken parachutes of milkweed seed to float across the late-summer landscape. The ornamental dried pods, turned at odd angles, remain on the stalks throughout the fall and winter.

In the past, milkweed silk was collected to use as quilt batting and as a wartime substitute for kapok.

I love the look of this plant at all seasons of the year, and always allow a few stalks to grow in my garden. As milkweed can be an invasive plant (or weed), I may ultimately come to regret this decision.

The Quilt Design

I did a number of freehand pencil drawings of stalks of milkweed pods before finally deciding on the composition for this quilt. I drew the contours of the pods so they were bumpy rather than sinuous, and full of the character I saw in the pods.

Two of the pods were drawn slightly open, revealing the seeds and tightly packed silk. Since the veining of the pods runs from base to tip, I drew seams in this direction, dividing each round pod into facets of varying widths. The stalks are interrupted at the nodes (or joints). I extended the seams that make the top and bottom of the nodes as gentle horizontal arcs. The arcs imply the movement of the wind and play against the strong verticals of the stalks in the overall composition.

The Fabric

In choosing fabrics for *Milkweed Pods*, I was guided by the pale, dull-green color of the pods, which fades to beige as the winter passes. The actual pods have a prickly surface and I interpreted this in fabric by choosing prints with some visual texture. I collected about a dozen fabrics for the pods.

The seeds were all cut from a single brown hand-dye with enough variation to make each seed a slightly different shade. I found a very narrow cotton seersucker fabric in my stash that was just the right texture for the tightly packed milkweed silk.

CHOOSING THE BACKGROUND FABRICS

To make the bright white seersucker really stand out, I decided to make the background of the quilt very dark. I chose a variety of fabrics in different types and scales of patterns, but none that were solid black. All of these deep-value fabrics contained colors and patterns that interacted with and complemented the fabrics in the pods. Some of the background fabrics had bits of purple or green or gold or brown, repeating or contrasting with some of the colors also found in the milkweed.

One of the background pieces included a pattern of large leaves drawn with fine lines and tiny white dots. The bright white in this fabric added sparkle to the surface of the quilt while relating visually to the white seersucker. This fabric—one of my favorites in recent years—included a wonderful mix of colors. The scale of the leaves in the print worked well with the other fabrics. The leaves also suggested other plant material in among the milkweed stalks, implied the time of year, contributed to the feeling of wind motion, and seemed like smaller versions of the pods. You'll see another bit of this fabric in *Cod* (page 52).

The purple at the lower left of the background may seem like a surprise. I selected the blue-purple hand-dyed shibori fabric because it provided a good complement to some of the mustard yellows. If you cover that purple, you will miss it. You will also find bits of purple in many of the other fabrics in the quilt. Actually, almost every fabric contains more than one color, as do the majority of the fabrics in my collection. (See pages 33, 76, and 94 for more on multicolor fabrics.)

I cut the stems of the milkweed plant from fabrics that were more yellow in color and more smoothly textured in pattern than those I used for the pods.

MAKING A STRIPE BEND

This is a very useful technique, especially in a quilt that features organic subject matter. Look at the pod on the upper right of the design. You'll see that I drew seams from the stem of the pod to its tip, dividing the pod into four or five longitudinal facets. I wanted to use a fabric with a striped pattern (with white dots) for the lower facet because the actual pods have many narrow parallel veins. If I used the fabric I selected as a single piece, the direction of the stripe would have aligned with the direction of the veins in only one area of the curved facet. The ruler-straight regularity of the stripe would have worked against the curved shape of the pod.

To make the stripe bend around the curve of the pod, I fractured the freezer-paper template for this facet into five pieces and changed the angle of the striped fabric slightly in each piece. This made the rigid stripe appear to bend around the pod. I used the same technique on the lower facet of the pod in the lower right corner of the design.

The Border

Some quilts need strong borders to set off the composition; other quilts work well with no borders at all. With *Milkweed Pods,* I felt that the addition of vertical strips as the side border would echo the strong verticals of the stalks. I interrupted them with continuations of some of the seaming lines coming from the pods, which broke the side borders and allowed me to use several different fabrics in a way that enhanced the overall composition. Interrupted borders on the top and bottom of the quilt gave me a chance to add interest to these areas with a greater variety of fabrics as well.

The Quilting

Free-motion machine quilting allowed me to add details to the design, providing me the chance to sketch a linear pattern on the pieced fabrics of the quilt top. I drew vein lines with slightly irregular and angled curves on the milkweed pods, interrupting each line of stitching with tiny angled branches to indicate the spiny nature of the pods. This stitching required "twitching" every few centimeters. I didn't want to do this stitching with a programmed embroidery stitch, because I didn't want the stitching to be that regular.

I quilted down the white seersucker with white cotton thread to throw the brown seeds into more relief. To flatten and unify the background, I quilted with black cotton thread in an overall pattern.

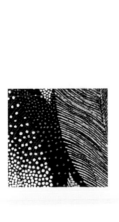

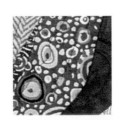

MAPLE LEAVES

Sunshine and Shadow: Sugar Maple Leaves, 79" x 62", © 1999 Ruth B. McDowell. Photo by John Nollendorf

H aving lived all my life in New England, the fall—with its wonderful hillsides of colorful leaves—is a time of year I always anticipate. My favorite tree is the sugar maple, with its yellow, orange, and red colors in fall and the familiar silhouette of the brownish-gray trunk and branches in winter. Sometimes the trees are tapped in late winter or early spring for the sap that is evaporated to make maple sugar. Later—with the first frost—the the cool green shade of summer transforms into the reds and golds of fall again.

I've made a number of quilts with the sugar-maple imagery. This time I used the tip of a branch of leaves in their autumn colors for my starting point. I chose the title from a traditional pattern, which may in turn be derived from the title of a hymn.

The Quilt Design

The drawing for this quilt originated with a close-up photograph I had taken the previous autumn. The leaves at the edge of the photograph were skewed in a curious way because of the shape of the camera lens, and I found I liked the effect. I maintained the distortion in the quilt design, but subdued the colors of the outside leaves. I wanted to keep the focus on the more natural shapes and brighter colors of the leaves in the center.

PIECING CONSIDERATIONS

It can be quite a puzzle to plan the piecing drawing for an overlapped image like this one. I decided to draw slightly curved seams in each leaf, along the lines of the major veins. These seams broke the leaves into

sections that reflected the skeleton of the leaf structure. By extending the seams past the edge of the leaf, it was possible to piece the sharp points on the tips of the leaves.

The edge of the leaf between the vein seams was best described by a curve. In almost every section of leaf, part of the curved edge had a fairly tight radius, reflecting the shape of the sinuses of the leaf edge. These tight radii would be very difficult to machine piece.

In working out the seamlines, I began with the forward-most leaf and worked my way back. I shifted the leaves a bit to slightly simplify the construction seams. The vein seams broke the image into smaller sections, and I drew the seamlines for the edges of the leaves and the shadows within these sections.

QUILT SIZE

The scale of the quilt was determined by the size I wanted the pieces to be. I knew I would be using many patterned fabrics, so I wanted pieces large enough to show off the prints. Working in a larger scale also gave the leaves more presence and kept the overall design spacious rather than fussy. The width of this quilt is 79", making the yellow-orange leaf in the center about 20" across, rather than the 4"–5" it actually was.

The Fabric

For each leaf, I gathered fabrics related to each other in hue. I used a different collection of fabrics for each leaf. Some leaves were more yellow, some were redder, some were lighter, and some duller. As I envisioned a bright and sunny fall day, there was the sunlight and shadow on the leaves to contend with as well. Some leaves required two related groups of fabrics, with one a shadow version of the other. It was crucial to access a wide range of different types and scales of patterned fabrics.

FABRIC DIALOGUE

As I chose, cut, and pinned more fabrics in place, the fabric choices got harder. I'd already made a lot of decisions. The next fabric needed to fit in with those already in place. The process was—as always—a dialogue between the available fabrics, the developing quilt, and the quiltmaker (me). By keeping an open mind, rather than trying to force the quilt into a preconceived direction, I usually achieve better results.

Selecting where to place the red and yellow leaves was a composition decision rather than a decision based on the original photograph. (Indeed, in a quilt of this kind, I often find it a good idea to dispense with the photograph altogether partway through the process.) At this point, I'd made enough color decisions to make the remaining choices based on the quilt in progress on my design wall.

The leaves formed a three-dimensional cluster on the end of a living branch, so I included a number of background fabrics with bright white in them to suggest the air flowing around the leaves. In addition, I chose background fabrics with patterns that implied other branches and trees behind the images in the foreground. Were I making a quilt with a collection of colored leaves *after* they had fallen to the ground, it would have been quite a different quilt—one lacking the shadows and the airy background, and with most of the leaves flat rather than tipped at various angles.

One of the border fabrics—a lighter, elegantly woven plaid—was particularly interesting when viewed up close. This fabric included a variety of reds and yellows less intense than the reds and yellows in the leaves. It was also light enough to keep the edge of the quilt fluid, but with areas dark enough to connect it to the dark areas in the center of the quilt. The geometry of the plaid made a pleasant counterpoint to the curves in the leaves, and set up the straight edge of the quilt's perimeter.

I added a square block in the bottom left corner to enliven a blank area, to balance the overall composition, and to reference a traditional quilt style. Other darkish plaid fabrics, all including colors to echo the leaves, filled out the border and framed the composition.

THOUGHTS ON WHAT MAKES A FABRIC "RIGHT"

Sometimes fabrics surprise us. In the yellow-orange leaf in the center of the quilt, I included some hand-dyed fabrics, some typical small-scale quilters' prints, and an orange and white plaid. The white plaid may seem improbable here, but if I replaced it with a solid orange fabric, the leaf would lose its sparkle. An orange fabric with a regular pattern of white polka dots maintained the sparkle but lacked the strong directional impact of the plaid. If I substituted an orange fabric with a random scattering of white daisies, the leaf missed the regular repeat of the polka dot or plaid. The straight geometry of the plaid also contrasted with the curves of the seaming. In other words, the orange and white plaid was the perfect choice.

The Border

I incorporated the border of the quilt inside the drawing of leaves, just as I did with *Pumpkins* (see pages 18–21). The abstract leaves overlapping the border were cut mostly from plaid fabrics of less color and intensity than the fabrics I had chosen for the interior leaves. These fabrics suggested additional leaves without being too obvious or intrusive. The branch I imagined was, after all, part of a much bigger tree that extended unseen well beyond the edge of the quilt.

I selected the fabrics for the linear borders to complement those I had already chosen for the maple leaves and background areas.

The Quilting

Sunshine and Shadow: Sugar Maple Leaves was free-motion quilted using quilting stitches to draw vein patterns on the leaves, and various overall patterns to flatten the background and border areas. Parts of the background were quilted with my favorite fan pattern, turned in different directions so as not to be too rigid. In a quilt such as this one, using such highly patterned fabrics, the quilting almost disappears as a line pattern, but does add different textures to the different parts of the design.

A RASH OF FLAMINGOES

You almost always see flamingoes in flocks rather than standing alone, and the imagery created by groups, flocks, and schools of animals, birds, and fish has always intrigued me. The similarities and differences between each figure, the relationship of one to the next, the visual repetition, the space in between, and the flow of the image all contribute to this visual fascination.

Traditional American quilts made from repeated pieced blocks attracted me to this medium from the start. While I do not construct many of my art quilts from identical repeated geometric units, I remain drawn to the idea of multiples.

It's hard to be serious about flamingoes, although ornithologists (and other flamingoes) might have a different view. I enjoy making quilts that make people smile, and I enjoyed giving each of these birds a slightly different personality.

A Rash of Flamingoes, 100" x 51", © 2000 Ruth B. McDowell

The Quilt Design

In drawing this flock, I chose mostly curved lines, overlapping and placing the birds in a variety of poses. The size of the quilt was determined both by the number of birds and the size of the pieces of fabric I wanted to use to make them.

DEVELOPING THE IMAGE LAYERS

I began the piecing diagram by drawing the bird in front first. In order to piece the sharp tips of the feathers on the back of this bird, I followed the curved seam of an edge of each feather in an arch downward toward the ground. This arching curve, a construction line, leads the eye up to the feathers on the back of the bird, and begins to integrate the shapes of the birds with the piecing of the background of the quilt. Most of the seam lines that break up the background of the quilt originate as construction seams coming from the birds.

After drawing the seams to piece the foremost flamingo, I moved back to the next bird, again extending curved seams downward from the tips of the edge feathers. These curved seams, made necessary by the piecing process, broke the quilt top into sewable sections. In addition, the network of seams united the birds, and the rest of the quilt, in a unique technical and visual way.

FRACTURING TO IMPLY DEPTH

Where a construction curve from one bird crossed a leg or the neck of a bird behind it, I drew a slight mismatch in the leg of the hindmost bird. This put more emphasis on the construction curve and made it more visually prominent. Fracturing the seam in the leg or neck of the second bird in this way made it appear to recede in the picture, because your eye picks out the continuous curve more quickly than the fractured one. I found the process much like playing with depth of field in photography. The foremost bird stayed in focus while the fractured lines of the birds in the background put them out of focus.

THOUGHTS ON QUILT SIZE

When I begin a new quilt drawing, I don't plan for the finished quilt to be a particular size to fit over the sofa. I make it the size the quilt needs to be to achieve the image I have in mind. I often remind people to check the dimensions of a quilt they see in a book, as it is difficult to visualize a quilt's scale from a small photograph. To give you a sense of the size of *this* quilt, the flamingo necks measure between $1^1/_4$" and $2^1/_2$" wide.

The Fabric

My pieced flamingoes exhibit a rather wider range of pinks than you would probably find in a single flock—a case of artistic license on my part. The pink fabrics included batiks, hand-dyes, vintage fabrics, 1930s reproduction fabrics, furnishing fabrics, and contemporary fabrics made specifically for quilters (I've never had a problem using fabrics of different weights and thicknesses). The many sources of pink fabric gave me many more shades of pink and more variety in types and scales of pattern than I could have found in fabrics from a single source.

JUNGLE FABRICS

Behind the flamingoes, I used fairly large pieces of four or five jungle fabrics, allowing the large-scale prints to imply heavy foliage. I think most viewers tend to focus on the area of the densest piecing, which, in this case, would be the smaller pieces in each of the flamingoes. Had I pieced many fabrics to form the jungle background, the jungle would have competed for attention with the birds.

Several of the large background prints had flecks of orange or pink in them, which picked up the pinks in the flamingoes and carried the color across the quilt.

BEACH FABRICS

I chose a number of brownish fabrics in a variety of scales and patterns to suggest a muddy beach. I was not trying to be literal with the choice of these background fabrics, but rather to imply a landscape environment for the flock. I also chose fabrics that made

interesting combinations with the colors and shapes of the flamingoes. I wanted to make certain that the flamingoes remained the focus of the piece, and were not overwhelmed by the background.

One fabric that "washed up" as I constructed the beach was a remnant of twill fabric originally intended for slipcovers or drapes. This fabric included a pattern of curved stripes in browns and blacks with some areas of light and dark shading. Despite the fact that it was a much larger, bolder pattern than the other beach fabrics I had selected, the fabric virtually leapt into my hand. Now that I think about it, I suspect this was because the light and dark curved stripes were visually reminiscent of the layers of curved feathers on the backs of the flamingoes.

THOUGHTS ON MULTICOLOR FABRICS

Fabrics that include multiple colors are much more useful in creating a visual transition between design elements than fabrics of a single hue. A painter often uses many colors in a single brushstroke, rather than dipping the brush in a single color. In a quilt, prints and plaids provide a similar benefit by including many colors in a single piece of fabric. Unfortunately, it is sometimes difficult to find good multicolor fabrics.

If you need a literal explanation for the presence of this fabric, I suppose you could say it represented beach grass, or seaweed, or molted flamingo feathers. It didn't matter to me what it "was" as long as the fabric worked visually. If I had used something more conventional in place of the curved stripe, the overall composition would have suffered and the resulting quilt would not have been nearly as interesting.

At the same time, the fifteen flamingoes made a bold enough image to stand up to the strong pattern in this particular fabric, which might well have overwhelmed a more delicate group.

The Border

I planned a pieced border for *A Rash of Flamingoes* for much the same reason I did for *Pumpkins* (pages 18–21), choosing different fabrics for different parts of the border design. One of the border fabrics—a lighter, streaky hand-dye with bits of green, yellow, pink, and red—had been in my fabric stash for some time. The colors in this fabric lightened the center of the top border, picked up other colors in the quilt, and brought the focus more into the center area. Because I couldn't resist the impulse, I used one piece of this fabric to suggest a topknot for one of these funny birds.

The Quilting

I free-motion quilted on the flamingoes to follow the pattern of the feathers, but not in-the-ditch. Using a pink variegated cotton thread, I stitched a similar feather pattern on the surface of the pieced flamingoes, offset from the piecing. By shifting the quilting line off the seamlines, I added lightness to the design, a sense of motion, and an additional linear pattern to the pieced surface. The background and beach areas were a bit more densely quilted to throw the flamingoes into relief.

■ ■ ■ ■ ■

When I finished quilting, I added the flamingo eyes as raw-edge machine appliqués. (The eyes were so small that piecing them in would have been impossible.) Actual flamingo eyes are pinkish yellow, almost the same color and value as the birds' feathers. From a distance, you can't see the eyes at all. I didn't want the eyes to disappear on my fabric birds, so I took the liberty of making them black. Although this may offend some ornithological purists, I think it is a better visual decision for *A Rash of Flamingoes*.

FRAGMENTS FROM AN ANCIENT DAWN

I have come back to trees again and again as subject matter for my quilts, and to be so connected to an ancient tree whose wood has become petrified seems magical to me. I find it fascinating that once—eons ago—the tree was wood,

In some cases, the pieces of petrified wood show the outside of the log where the bark once existed, as well as the lengthwise pattern of the tree cells. In other cases, the rock has split across the grain of the wood, so you can see the pattern of the annual rings. Sometimes the species of tree can be identified by carefully studying the fossil.

Annular rings are a tree's calendar—a record of the influence of moisture, temperature, and sunlight on the growth of that tree in a given year. Petrified wood is a record of ancient climate cast in stone.

FROM PHOTOGRAPH TO DRAWING TO QUILT
I took many photographs at the Petrified Forest National Monument in Arizona when I visited there several years ago. One photograph, a detail of a small ruined building composed of these stones, led to the drawing for this quilt. I selected that particular photograph because of the composition, the strong play of light and shadow, the colors, and the mixture of one spectacular cross-sectioned piece among several longitudinal chunks and fragments.

The petrified pieces were imbedded in mortar. I have really mixed feelings about the use of such treasures as building material. Petrified wood seems much too precious for such humble use. But the deed had been done. I thought perhaps a quilt would get people to look at this stone in a different way.

The Quilt Design

I decided on irregularly curved and angled seams, all drawn freehand to maintain the quality of the lines I saw in the stone. The piecing would be complicated, so I made little attempt to divide the image into sewable sections. In the end, it required many partial seams and elaborate sewing sequences.

The design didn't require a classical border; I chose to float the image on a narrow, flat "mat" as I wanted to create some space between the central stone image and the binding.

The Fabric

I looked for fabrics to recall the colors and textures of the actual pieces of stone. The cross-section slice was much lighter in color and smoother in texture than the longitudinal chunks. At the very center was a small hole— a check in the heart of the slice of wood. The cross section revealed hints of blues, roses, purples, grays, and browns. I used several hand-dyed fabrics, a commercial tie-dye-type fabric, and some very pale watercolor-like patterned fabrics. Some were used both right and wrong side up for their slightly different values.

The lengthwise chunks of petrified wood had some much rougher and darker surfaces, as well as some smoother areas. A few beautiful hand-dyed fabrics were helpful here, along with some printed pieces.

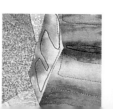

TEXTURE AND PATTERN

Several chunks of stone in the center right area of the quilt included rough bluish areas that called for a bit more pattern. I found just the fabric I needed in the reverse side of a blue and white print with touches of yellow and orange. I had discovered this fabric in Japan in 1993, and if you look very carefully, you'll see some rather Pre-Raphaelite imagery of trees and knights and maidens in it. I used the parts of the fabric I needed to get the textures and colors I saw in the stone, at the same time minimizing the figures to keep them from being distracting.

I used three different small-scale textural prints as the mortar that filled the spaces between the stones, and as the ground.

THOUGHTS ON PRESSING SEAM ALLOWANCES

The way seam allowances are pressed can have a dramatic impact on how a piece looks. Pressing seam allowances to one side or the other of each seam creates a padding that raises one fabric piece above the other. Although traditional piecing gives rules to follow, not many quiltmakers actually *look* at the differences the pressing direction makes on the finished quilt. Pressing the seam allowances open is also an option many quilt-makers don't explore.

In general, I press the seam allowances toward the piece of fabric I want to come forward in the quilt, or I press them open when I want both fabrics to appear in the same plane. In *Fragments From an Ancient Dawn,* for example, I pressed the seam allowances under the pieces of petrified wood to raise them away from the mortar. In *Reflections* I pressed the seams in the water reflections open because I wanted the fabrics to appear in the same plane rather than one in front of the other as they would appear if these seam allowances were pressed to one side (see page 45).

As I piece, I pay careful attention to how I want to use the seam allowances, especially because the padding created by pressing seam allowances to one side or the other is amplified by the addition of the quilting stitches.

Rethinking Tradition

I believe that the traditional practice of pressing seam allowances to one side evolved for two reasons. A hand-pieced (running stitch) seam can be fairly weak. It is most easily mended if both seam allowances are turned to one side rather than pressed open. Additionally, bat-ting fibers can migrate through a seam that is pressed open; the spaces between stitches are greater than those between the woven threads of the fabrics.

To some degree, machine-pieced seams minimize both of these problems. The type of fibers in the batting also has an impact, with migration more likely with some poly-ester battings. However, if you choose to press seam allowances open, be sure to sew the seams with a short stitch length (2.0 or smaller) to prevent whatever batting you plan to use from "bearding" or migrating through the seam.

While it is tradition to press seam allowances away from light fabrics to prevent shadowing, this pale shadow can sometimes be used to your advantage. I don't often find pressing seam allowances toward a light piece to be a problem, and I find the chance to give visual depth to a quilt a more important aspect in making these decisions.

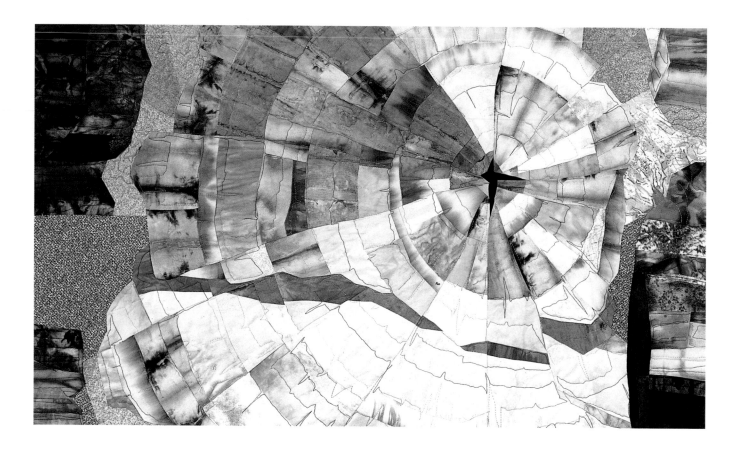

The Quilting

I drew additional texture on the rocks by free-motion quilting with solid and variegated cotton threads. I quilted the cross-sectioned area to suggest the pattern of annual rings, and stipple quilted the mortar densely to flatten it and to raise the stones.

The black and white variegated cotton thread I used (50-weight DMC Machine Broder/Embroidery) has a distance of about 1 meter between the blackest black and the whitest white. Notice how the quilted line appears and disappears in the annual rings depending on whether the value of the quilting thread contrasts with or matches the value of the fabric it is stitched across. To choose a quilting thread that will show prominently, use a different value than that of the fabric; the *value* is more important than the *color*. With a variegated thread, I am not in precise control of how it will appear, but I like that element of chance. See *Cod* (page 56) for another use of this variegated thread.

Although *Fragments From an Ancient Dawn* began as a fairly literal adaptation of a photograph, the resulting quilt has much more meaning for me. It references trees and stone and the passage of time. It references the uses man sometimes makes of natural treasures, treating them as ordinary building material, then abandoning the building to time and the elements.

I love the different visual textures in the quilt, and the beautiful circular shape of the cross section with its small, dark void in the middle.

Many people have told me they find *Fragments From an Ancient Dawn* a very meditative image, whether they are responding to the tree, the stone, or just the combination of shapes around the pale, calm, circular shape.

IKAT ANEMONES

Ikat Anemones, 31" x 38", © 2001 Ruth B. McDowell

I love the bright red, blue-purple, pink, and white colors; ferny foliage; and dark centers of the anemone called *Monarch de Caen*. When it shows up in the greenhouses, this colorful flower always reminds me that spring is just around the corner.

The Quilt Design

After making a drawing of a few flowers, I began working on a piecing design. For this quilt, I chose to use curved seams and to focus primarily on the flowers.

Beginning with the foremost flower, I drew sweeping curves through the center of the petals, curving the seamlines upward in a cupped shape much like the flowers themselves. The curved seams reinforced the three-dimensional shape of the flowers and began to split the entire design into wedgelike sections that met in the flower centers.

PLANNING CURVED SEAMS

The curved seams splitting the petals made the petals easier to piece. In most cases, half a petal was sewn to the background pieces, and then the sections were joined with long simple seams.

This was a much easier process than sewing a tight U-shaped petal as a single piece, and gave me the chance to vary the fabric in the two half-petals or to slightly change the angle of the pattern in the fabric. The curves in the foremost flowers also deliberately fractured the petals and stems behind them, which—to my eye—increased the sense of depth.

FRACTURING TO IMPLY DEPTH

You can see this best in the long stem on the flower near the right edge of the quilt. Had I made that stem a continuous line, it would have assumed too much importance as a design element. Fracturing the line of the stem caused it to recede. This was a conscious design decision, and not the result of sloppy sewing.

To keep the image from becoming too complex, I intentionally eliminated the leaves and the ring of foliage that grow on the actual flower stems.

The Fabric

I chose two woven-cotton ikat fabrics for the petals: the red one is from India and the blue one is from the Mekong River area of Vietnam. These fabrics are more loosely woven than typical quilt fabrics. I added a few other red and blue fabrics for variety.

The petals in the center of an anemone shade almost to white, and are covered by a ring of dark stamens and a dark ovary. I looked for a fabric with dark spots on white to make the stamens. I *found* white spots on dark in the right scale in a Dutch-wax indigo-dyed cotton fabric.

Although the colorway was the reverse of what I wanted, the scale and texture of the fabric worked. I split the ring of petals into wedges, planning a slight mismatch of the edges where the pieces joined to make the ring seem more fluid, and not so much like a bullseye.

BACKGROUND FABRICS

To give the impression of a garden in early spring, I ransacked my fabric stash for some light-background, large-scale prints with elements of bright spring green. I found three scraps of vintage 1960s decorator remnants with bright white backgrounds. The scale of these prints was good, the colors were right, and the white backgrounds added the airiness I wanted. One of the fabrics even had some purple tulips—frequently seen as garden companions to anemones.

I added several more contemporary quilting fabrics with similar colors. Many of the background fabrics contained bits of blue or red or green. One had a rather regular pattern of dots on a dark green background. The scale and the regular repeat of the dots had a different rhythm than the other prints.

REPETITION OF COLOR

The white backgrounds in the decorator fabrics repeated the white background in the Dutch-wax fabric I used for the stamens. I had quite a collection of Dutch-wax indigo-dyed cottons, and selected several possibilities.

I needed something to tie the white and indigo fabrics to the others in the background and found a Dutch-wax fabric with a green over-dyed stripe in my stash. (It came that way; I don't dye fabric.) You can see this green stripe in the border on the right edge of the quilt. This fabric was the key to making this overall collection of fabric work. I pieced it into the quilt at a slight angle, opposite to the angle of the anemone stems. This design decision did have construction consequences—part of the left and bottom borders then had bias edges, but with this fairly firmly woven fabric and careful handling, the quilt came out fine.

THOUGHTS ON PATTERN IN FABRIC

In a composition such as *Ikat Anemones*, the type and scale of pattern in the fabrics is at least as important as the color. A design like this requires an eclectic and varied fabric stash to draw from.

The Border

In this quilt, as with several others in the book, I planned the piecing lines I needed to make the flowers first. Once these were drawn, I drew additional lines to complete the composition and to frame the image, creating an irregular border in the process.

Since the flower image was loose and placed asymmetrically, I needed border fabrics that would balance and complement the off-center arrangement.

A narrow outer border of a single Dutch-wax cotton brought the size of the quilt to the right proportion for its center image. The dark binding fabric had a sprinkling of red spots to pick up the reds in the center flowers.

The Quilting

I quilted the shapes of the pieced petals, loosely echoing the flower shapes (but not in-the-ditch), using the same black-to-white variegated thread that I used in *Cod* (see page 56) and *Fragments From an Ancient Dawn* (see page 38). I drew more quilted anemones in the lighter areas at the upper left, while a tight meandering quilting pattern added texture to the stamens in the pieced flowers. Slightly wavy parallel lines at various angles (a design suggested by the printed striped pattern of the green border fabric on the right) were used to quilt the area below the flowers. More elaborate quilting was not needed because of the highly patterned fabrics in the quilt.

■ ■ ■ ■ ■

By the time I finished this quilt, I had used up every bit of the three drapery fabrics I had found to begin the background design. I had probably had those fabrics for 20 years before I made this quilt. They weren't fabrics I particularly liked. (They weren't from *my* slipcovers!)

It intrigues me how the quilts I make are intimately tied to the fabrics I happened to have available to me at the time. If I began this quilt again, it would look completely different because I now have a different collection of fabric to draw from.

The fabrics in *Ikat Anemones* represent a point in time in my quiltmaking. They came from many different sources: some I purchased myself, some were remnants given to me by others, some were leftovers from clothing or furnishing projects.

REFLECTIONS

Reflections, 23" x 58¹/₂", © 2002 Ruth B. McDowell

I don't make quilts on commission. Instead, I allow myself the great luxury of making the quilts I want to make when the proper moment arrives.

I also tremendously enjoy teaching, mostly because of the people I meet. A typical class may include students ranging in age from 20 to 80 who come from a wide variety of backgrounds and life experiences. In June 2002, I had the delightful experience of teaching in Denmark. Of course, I went home with many visual images to inspire me.

ARCHITECTURE AND OUTLINES

Copenhagen has the most fascinating and eclectic collection of church steeples I've ever seen. The steeple featured in *Reflections* has a spiral staircase around the outside. Spiral staircases are a favorite of mine since I have a wonderful two-story spiral staircase in my 1840 house here in Massachusetts.

I saw the Copenhagen steeple one sunny morning while out for a boat ride. On a trip along one of the canals, I spotted a lovely red-masted wooden boat beside a small blue rowboat.

The little rowboat was clinker-built; that is, built with overlapped planks like the clapboards on a house. The profile of those overlapped planks formed an elongated stair-step pattern—the same outline, on a different scale, as the spiral staircase on the steeple. While many other people overlook them, these types of visual parallels fascinate me.

The Quilt Design

I adapted the drawing of the boats from a photograph I took that morning in Copenhagen. I needed to do a great deal of adapting to simplify the boats enough to sew them. Behind the boats, I added pared-down versions of the buildings along the canal. I pulled a drawing of the church steeple from another photo, and dropped it in behind the buildings. I recognize that this decision did some injustice to the streets of Copenhagen, but I considered it an example of artistic license used to fulfill my vision.

The composition became a tall, narrow rectangle to accommodate the images. I liked the way my eye moved among the verticals of the steeple and the masts. The use of a subtle plaid for sky added another set of vertical lines.

The Fabric

Fabric selection for *Reflections* presented a number of challenges. I needed to find fabrics reminiscent of stone, tile, stucco, and glass for the buildings, in the browns, reds, and ochres that said "Copenhagen" to me.

The top windows on the large brown building to the left reflected more light, while the windows on the two lower stories were slightly darker. In addition, the windows had very small panes. I found a piece of old drapery fabric that had the right kind of pattern to suggest the windowpanes. I used the fabric right side up in the windows on the two lower floors and wrong side up on the top floor to make those windows slightly lighter.

ARCHITECTURAL DETAILS

The steeple had a great deal of architectural detail, with balusters and arches and fancy stonework. In my stash, I found a small stripe for the balusters. A brown and black printed fabric with a pattern of squarish ovals worked well for the arches, although I had to carefully cut and resew the fabric to get the ovals in approximately the right places. The golden finial at the top of the steeple was added with hand appliqué.

REFLECTIONS AND SHADOWS

Next I searched for fabrics to make the reflections in the canal at the lower part of the quilt, as well as fabrics to make the boats. I pressed the seams in the water-reflection fabrics open. Reflections are a surface phenomenon—both fabrics should appear in the same plane rather than one in front of the other as it would appear if these seam allowances were pressed to one side. (See page 37 for more on pressing seams.)

The little blue rowboat presented a quandary. To suggest the clinker-built nature, I was willing to piece the sides of the boat from narrow strips of blue—one strip per plank. However, I needed a shadow line on each plank to really show it off. I could have added the shadows with a marker. I could have tried to make the shadows by quilting with dark thread (although that probably would not have made a strong enough line). I decided I would rather—if I could—make the shadow on each plank with a printed fabric, so I headed off to search my fabric stash.

On the shelf, I found a very large-scale floral with dark and light blue among its many colors. I discovered I could cut this fabric selectively so that each piece included both the dark and the light blue—that is, both the plank and its shadow. The planks on the left side of the rowboat were cut with more dark blue, while those on the sunlit right side were cut with more light blue. There was a certain absurdity in this process, which strikes me as I write about it, and now and then when I'm actually doing it. I can't explain to anyone who isn't a quiltmaker why I go to this much trouble, except to say that the search for the perfect fabric is rather a lot of fun.

There were some smooth, curved seams in the water: construction lines that slightly fractured the reflection of the blue rowboat as it would be broken by the ripples in the water. The fabrics I selected for the water were streakier, with somewhat murkier colors and in slightly softer patterns than those used above. These fabrics barely suggested the elements they reflected. The light diagonal streaks at the lower right were, in the photograph, ripples caused by the bow wave of the sightseeing boat. They made a strong diagonal in the quilt—a good element in the composition because they were angled in opposition to the diagonals in the perspective of the buildings.

The Border

To understand the issues in planning a border for this quilt, cut four strips of white paper and place them on the edges of the center rectangle, masking out the border. This is how the quilt top looked when I finished piecing the central image.

I felt this pieced scene needed a bit more space around the image before I added the binding. The issue of scale determined the width of the borders. I also wanted to bring a little more ochre and red into the lower half of the quilt to balance those colors in the boats and buildings. I did this by piecing three small strips, cut across a red and ochre striped fabric, into the border to balance the composition.

To frame the sky at the top of the quilt, I looked for fabrics with an "open" feel to repeat the colors I had used in the central image. I was looking especially for larger-scale prints with enough white so that the sky wouldn't appear to be trapped in a box. I found one such fabric in a streaky blue and white large-scale print that probably began life as a dressmaking fabric.

I needed to carry some red into the upper right border as well. A hand-stenciled white fabric, with a pattern of random crisscrossed bars that shifted from red to blue, was the perfect scale. It brought flecks of red to the top corner of the quilt and added interest to the large open piece of sky. In addition, the red bars on this fabric repeated the red masts on the largest boat. Now that I think of it, red bars on white is the reverse of the white bars on red that appear on the Danish flag. That flag festooned a memorable birthday celebration thrown for me by the quilters in Vammen, Denmark.

The Quilting

I used quilting to draw rigging on the sailboats, stitching over the lines twice to thicken them. I did this stitching with the feed dogs up to help keep the lines of stitching straight.

I created free-motion quilting patterns to further define the building materials on the architecture in the quilt, and stitched in-the-ditch along the seams of the boats. I stitched slightly wavy lines for ripples in the canal, and used my favorite fan-quilting pattern to flatten the sky. To my mind, the curves of the fans suggested puffy clouds, and softened the linear plaid of the sky fabric. The curves also complemented the straight seams of the architecture.

SUMMER LILY

Summer Lily, 58" x 70", © 2002 Ruth B. McDowell

C anada Lily, or *Lilium canadensis*, grows in wet meadows, borders, and woodlands in Canada and the northeastern United States, and in the mountains of the
Southeast. The flowers are usually yellow, but can also be orange or red, and measure
up to 3" wide. As many as sixteen to twenty flowers can grow candelabra-style on a
plant that can reach 5' tall. This is a truly wonderful, but rather scarce, wildflower.

The Quilt Design

I designed *Summer Lily* from a series of photographs taken by my friend Verena Rybicki. I began with a drawing about half the size of the final quilt, finding this easier to work with than a full-scale sketch. When I was satisfied with the drawing, I enlarged it on a copier to the size I wanted for the piecing diagram. With an image as complicated as this, I had many avenues to consider in terms of planning the piecing. I could have focused on a single flower, but the magnificence of the whole stalk really appealed to me.

PIECING CONSIDERATIONS

I considered using curved seaming—a more naturalistic choice since the petals of the lily are actually curved—but I decided on a combination of straight seams and inset-corner, angled seams instead. The energy of the straight-line segments seemed to make the image more dynamic, and at the same time more abstract.

By increasing the scale of the flowers to more than 20" (larger-than-life in scale) I was able make the piecework image I had in mind with good-sized pieces of fabric. I realized that these larger pieces would better show off the wonderful fabrics I planned to use. I was also able to include a lot more pieced detail than would have been possible with flowers closer to life size. For example, the dark cinnamon-brown stamens made a bold statement with the yellow petals, and I was able to piece them in.

The leaves of Canada lily grow in whorls, and I included one whorl in the pieced design. I pruned away a few leaves and other plant parts that appeared to confuse the overall image.

DEVELOPING THE LAYERS

I began the piecing design for this three-dimensional image by setting up the piecing lines I'd need to make the foremost flower, in this case the large flower in the lower right area of the design. I worked my way back progressively into the image, taking each element in turn. I discovered that I needed to carry a seamline from one side of the petal tip out across the background in order to piece the sharp petal tip. If you look carefully, you will see a seam that runs from the leftmost petal of the first flower and continues as a diagonal seam all across the quilt to the left edge.

The large flower at the top came next—again with long seams extending from each petal tip—and then the large

flower on the lower left. These seamlines were an important factor in constructing the quilt, splitting it into sewable sections. They also fractured the elements further back in the design. I deliberately planned slight mismatches in the stems and leaves where they were split by the seams from the flowers. To my eye, these slight mismatches pulled the stems and leaves slightly out of focus, and pushed them back visually. The flowers appeared to be in focus, while the leaves and stems blurred.

There was an underlying structure to the piecing of this quilt that derived from the structure of the lily. Even if you don't see or understand that when you view the quilt, it is an important part of its design.

The Fabric

I had a collection of golden-yellow fabrics waiting on the shelf when I began this quilt. Some were quilting fabrics and a few were curtain or slipcover fabrics. Another, a scrap of tablecloth, had areas of darker dots that reminded me of the dots on the actual lily petals. Two yellow prints had green leaves, which I fussy-cut to make a sepal where the top of the flower joined the stem. I chose darker, duller yellows for the flowers toward the back of the stalk than I chose for the flowers in the foreground.

A rich cinnamon-colored twill made great stamens, with the pattern in the fabric suggesting pollen grains. I had a striped fabric that worked for the stems of the stamens, and a light green drapery fabric I cut up for the pistils.

Because the stamens were rather dark in contrast with the petals, I wanted to strategically place other dark fabrics, both for balance and to lead the eye around the quilt. I used two very dark green prints (both with light flecks) for the leaves. These two greens were darker than the real leaves, but necessary to the balance of the composition.

BACKGROUND FABRICS

I used blue fabrics behind the golden-yellow lilies because they provided the complementary color, and therefore intensified the flowers. Actually, I used everything from turquoise to purple in this area, and a great range of different prints as well. The little green triangles in one purple fabric seemed to dance among the larger pieces to set up a playful rhythm.

THOUGHTS ON BACKGROUND FABRICS

I consider being able to compose the background of my quilt with the same care I use on the foreground one of the great boons of piecing over traditional appliqué, which typically relies on a single background fabric. The variety of fabrics inherent in piecing adds a tremendous amount of visual interest and—to me—produces a much richer surface.

The Border

Once the pattern of straight and inset-corner seams for the whole plant was established, I began to consider whether or not the quilt required a border. While some of my art quilts don't have any border at all, I felt this image needed one to strengthen the outside edge of the composition. I decided on a border built inside the drawing rather than one added to the outside because I thought the lily image was a good scale for the size of the quilt I was working on. Adding a border *outside* the lily drawing would have made the scale of the flowers too small for the ultimate size of the quilt.

I made the decision to fit the border between the already-established seamlines. This allowed me to break the border into a number of different fabrics, and to select the right fabric for each spot. I drew a border with a broader outer band, and a narrower band next to the center image. I planned corner squares for the more open, upper corners, but not in the lower corners where the piecing was denser.

I chose the border fabrics to complete the composition and frame the piece without confining it. I had a very large-scale curtain fabric from Holland with a lot of pure white background, green "leaves," and some colorful spots. I loved the way the color and scale of this fabric looked with the rest of the quilt. I used the whole piece of fabric, and then added some other soft greens to the outer border.

I paired a green Kaffe Fassett smaller-scale print with little bits of yellow and purple, and a green polka dot to make up part of the inner border. I made the narrow inner border at the top of the quilt from a feed-sack fabric I found in my stash after I had used up the other two fabrics.

For the bottom border area, I introduced a Kaffe Fassett leafy print with a Swiss chard pattern to suggest the leafy habitat in which the Canada lily grows.

In many cases, the image of the lily ran over the border. This kind of border was much looser in feeling than many traditional quilt borders, in that it framed the piece and completed the composition without imprisoning the lily in a rigid box. As a result it made the quilt more accessible visually and gave it room to breathe.

 THOUGHTS ON RUNNING OUT OF FABRIC

To me, running out of a fabric always makes for a better quilt in the end, although it can cause heart failure at the time! The necessary introduction of other, carefully chosen fabrics can greatly enrich the overall quilt. In the case of *Summer Lily*, I liked the quilt much better with the feed-sack border piece than I would have without it. I think the high contrast in the feed-sack print works better with the dark areas in the quilt than my original choice for fabric would have.

The Quilting

Because of the amount of pattern in the fabrics, the machine quilting did not show significantly. The background and borders were quilted entirely in variegated yellow cotton thread in an overall fan pattern reminiscent of traditional fan-patterned hand quilting. The variegated yellow thread was light to medium in value, as were most of the fabrics in the background, so the quilting thread wasn't prominent.

I started the arcs of the fan pattern from the top of the quilt, so the curves echo the downward handing bells of the flowers. I quilted on the leaves and flowers to add detail and vein lines.

COD

Cod, 113" x 64", © 2002 Ruth B. McDowell

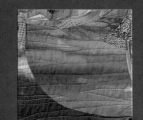

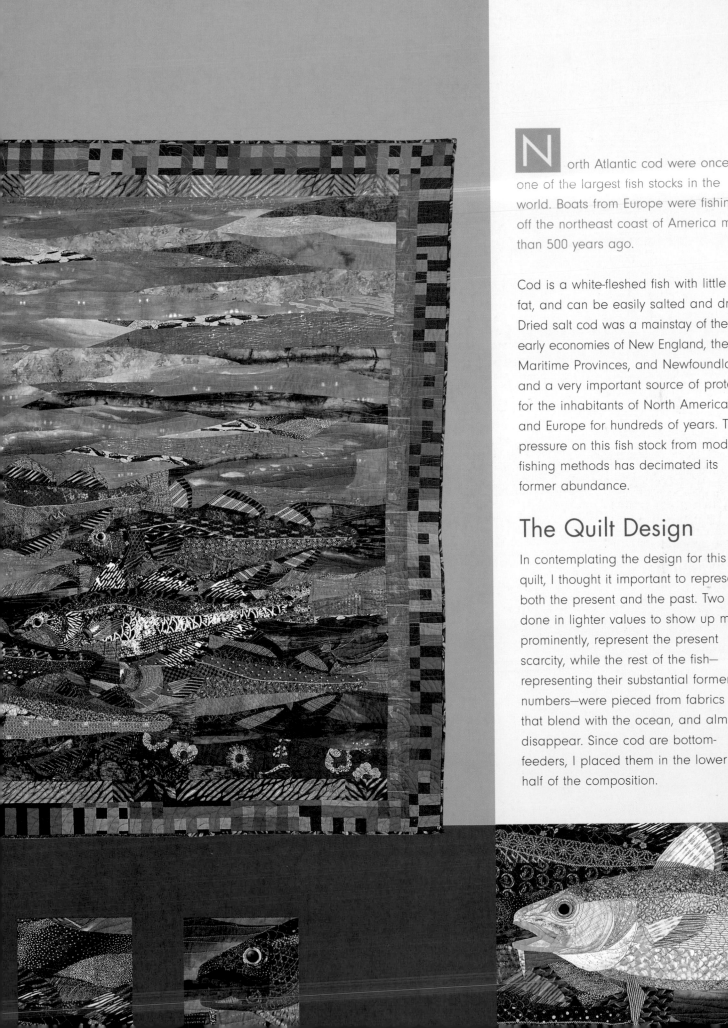

orth Atlantic cod were once one of the largest fish stocks in the world. Boats from Europe were fishing off the northeast coast of America more than 500 years ago.

Cod is a white-fleshed fish with little fat, and can be easily salted and dried. Dried salt cod was a mainstay of the early economies of New England, the Maritime Provinces, and Newfoundland, and a very important source of protein for the inhabitants of North America and Europe for hundreds of years. The pressure on this fish stock from modern fishing methods has decimated its former abundance.

The Quilt Design

In contemplating the design for this quilt, I thought it important to represent both the present and the past. Two fish, done in lighter values to show up more prominently, represent the present scarcity, while the rest of the fish—representing their substantial former numbers—were pieced from fabrics that blend with the ocean, and almost disappear. Since cod are bottom-feeders, I placed them in the lower half of the composition.

I drew one fish using curved seams, since that gave me the best representation of the shape of the cod. I shifted and redrafted that first fish drawing to create the other fish in the school. This was not a repeated block in the classical sense since the fish were overlapped and shifted in an irregular way, but rather a use of multiple images that reflects my ties to traditional repeated block quilts. I wanted a more irregular placement of the fish than would have resulted from a repeated geometric unit.

PIECING CONSIDERATIONS

Getting the image of the school I wanted required a very complicated method of piecing the codfish. I sewed parts of several fish together, leaving open seams, and then added other fish parts, went back to finish the partial seams, and added yet other fish. There were no clean, complete units to sew, as there would have been with repeated blocks.

I drew the seams within one fish to delineate the different parts—fins, gill covers, lips, and so on—as well as the areas of different values or textures. Each fin, for instance, contained three pieces: the darker piece next to the body, followed by a lighter piece with a streaky texture, and ending with a darker, striped tip. To give the fish some coherence, all the fins on a single fish were cut from the same three fabrics.

The Fabric

To produce the design I had in mind, I chose fabrics for the cod that were much more restricted in color, value, and pattern than the mix of fabrics I usually work with in my quilts. The selected fabrics (all cottons) included a number of quilting fabrics—several of them Japanese—as well as furnishing and other decorator fabrics, woven patterns, and vintage prints. The color palette was chosen to reflect the cold North Atlantic waters.

I chose not to use metallic fabrics in the quilt. I don't really like the look of metallic fabrics, or fabrics with metallic paint on them. I decided to see if I could make the fish shine without them.

OCEAN FABRICS

The fabrics for the upper ocean waters were much less detailed in pattern than the ones I had chosen for the fish, and included several purchased hand-dyed fabrics. In the lower part of the quilt, I used one printed fabric for ocean that had tiny dots of various colors, suggesting fish eggs or larva or plankton. (Ocean water is never empty of life!) The fabrics below the school of fish represented the ocean floor.

FISH FABRICS

I chose a group of fabrics for each fish that would tie together visually while making each fish slightly different from the next. At the same time, the fabrics for an individual fish were selected to represent the textures and values on an actual fish—for example, darker on the back, and lighter on the belly.

An important design feature on each cod was a prominent, light swim line running along the body. Rather than piecing this very narrow line, I *stitched* the swim line on each fish when I had finished the quilt top, but before layering the top with the batting and backing. I used white cotton thread and a programmed feather stitch on my Pfaff sewing machine to do this. I varied the width of the feather stitch, making it wider in the middle of the body and narrowing it to the tail. If I had done this stitching as quilting—that is, after I had assembled the top, batting, and backing—the swim line would have sunk down into the fish, rather than staying up on the surface.

The Border

The relatively simple border on *Cod* was designed to leave some space around the school, to add some crisp geometry to complement the many curves, to finish the outside edge of the composition, and to tweak the color composition. For the top and bottom, I used bands of shibori fabrics hand-dyed in diagonal patterns that reminded me of ripple patterns on the surface of the ocean and in sand. I had two fat quarters of this fabric—not enough to cut two bands over 100" long.

Knowing that I would need to piece strips to get the length I needed, I decided to make the piecing an intentional part of the design. I cut some squares and some strips of different lengths from the two fat quarters. When seaming the pieces together, I changed the direction of the diagonals to angle up and down. This made a much more interesting border than the one I would have made had I had enough fabric to cut a single long strip.

The Quilting

The quilting on the codfish was an important, but subtle, part of the design. I chose to free-motion machine quilt a pattern of scales on each fish using a black to white variegated DMC's Machine Broder/Embroidery 50-weight cotton thread. The transition from black to white on this thread covered about 36". Starting at the head of each fish and continuing toward the tail, I stitched rows of scales, quilting from back to belly and back again, until I had quilted the entire body. Each scale was between $1/2$" and $3/4$" in size.

GEOMETRIC PRINTS FOR CONTRAST

The fabrics for the other borders were crisp geometric prints chosen to contrast with the gentle curves of the piecing seams. I chose two Marimekko screen prints: one with blue and green squares, and another of slate blues with reds and golds. The reds and golds complemented all the blues in the quilt.

The square elements, both in the Marimekko fabrics and in the pieced shibori borders, refer back to traditional quilts. I often include squares, sawtooth elements, four-patches, or nine-patches in my designs, to honor the many women whose quilts inspired me to begin making quilts in the first place.

Because I used this variegated thread with such a distance from black to white, the quilting in the rows of scales shifted from black to gray to white to gray and back to black again in vertical bands 1" to 2" wide. This added a very slight visual ripple along the length of the fish.

I used dark thread in the bobbin when I quilted this quilt. The backing on the quilt, a shaded Marimekko cotton, showed off the quilting pattern more clearly; indeed, it looks like a traditional wholecloth quilt with a quilted school of codfish. At the upper back of the quilt and on the casing, I printed a list of the Evans family schooners, some of my fishing and shipbuilding ancestors from Exploits, Newfoundland.

FISH EYES

After finishing the quilting, I decided to add buttons for the codfish eyes. Although I had pieced in eyes for the fish, they didn't show up enough. I embellished the fish by sewing a small flat black plastic button on top of a large mother-of-pearl button for each eye. Since the mother-of-pearl buttons were slightly concave, they caught the light in wonderful ways, with different eyes shining at different times and from different perspectives.

THOUGHTS ON QUILTING

I quilted *Cod* on a Pfaff 7570, dropping the feed dogs and using a darning foot. It's awkward to quilt a large quilt on most home sewing machines because of the small amount of space under the arm of the machine. Although *Cod* is a long quilt, it's only 64" wide, so I was able to reach into the center from the top and bottom edges.

See page 12 for tips on machine quilting.

■ ■ ■ ■ ■

Cod is a quilt that is much more spectacular in life than it appears in a photograph. This seems true for many of my quilts. It is partly an issue of scale: the quilts need to be seen full size; that's one of the reasons I made them that size in the first place. But it's also an issue of the fabric medium. Fabrics have a presence and a warmth totally different from paint or photography. As a result, many people respond to quilts in a very personal way.

The Schooner Change, 67½" x 46½", © 2002 Ruth B. McDowell

One set of my great-grandparents, Percival Manuel (b. 1858) and Luciana Evans (b. 1862), came from the area of the Exploits Islands in Newfoundland. Percival and Luciana left Newfoundland in 1891 and moved south, eventually settling in Lynn, Massachusetts. Many of their relatives still live in Newfoundland.

The Manuel and Evans families had lived in Newfoundland for many years, fishing for cod in the warmer months, and salting and drying it on brushwood flakes along the rocky shore.

Both families built boats and fishing schooners as well, often over the winters. The Manuels built more than 100 schooners over the years, and the Evans family at least 40. Robert Evans built the schooner *Change,* the subject of this quilt, in 1909, for owners G. J. Carter and A. W. Picott. Its size was listed as 55 tons. The name *Change* referred to a change in government. The *Change* was the first of the Evans schooners built of mill-sawn lumber. All previous Evans schooners—at least 39 of them—were built from lumber sawed by hand from tree trunks. They were tough men and strong women on that island all those years ago.

The Quilt Design

A number of snapshots taken at Exploits in 1912 appear in our family photo album, including photographs of two of the Evans's schooners under sail. In planning this quilt, I wanted to combine a number of elements from these photographs in a single composition.

If I had drawn the harbor at Exploits as I saw it in the photographs, with the schooner in the harbor, the image of the schooner would have been very small. I wanted to show the ship at a much larger size, so I settled on the concept of a picture in a picture. I put the schooner image in a frame, and then set the framed image in a larger setting, suggesting the harbor of Exploits. (Actually, I combined images from several different photographs to draw the harbor, rather than picking a single vantage point.) At that time, the harbor was completely ringed by wharves, boats, flakes, and buildings of various sorts. No one lives there full time anymore.

Because I didn't want to confine the schooner in a tight box (it is, after all, a vessel of the open sea), I let some of the farther points of land interrupt the picture frame.

The Fabric

I selected a single fabric for the sails, and other fabrics for the hull and cabin. I planned to piece in the masts and add some additional lines and rigging with stitching.

I broke the water with horizontal lines, choosing a number of blue to greenish-blue fabrics for the sea to reflect the color of the water on a sunny day. A large-scale blue and white fabric suggested the billowing clouds in the bright sky without being photographically realistic.

THOUGHTS ON PRINTED FABRIC

I have a strong personal aversion to using printed fabric that resembles a photographic image. I'm not making photographs; I'm making quilts. Even though I often work from photographs, I'm after an impressionistic fabric image, not a photographically realistic one.

USING FRAMES

I composed the frame around the schooner from a number of fabrics, which I selected after many of the other fabric decisions were made. I wanted a slightly heavier border below and on the right side of the ship to balance the overall composition, and selected a beige, brown, and blue plaid. The lighter beige bits added a pleasingly regular visual rhythm. The plaid related to the other plaids I used elsewhere in the quilt.

On the left side of the frame, now broken into two parts, I wanted to use a different fabric than the plaid I had used on the other areas of the frame. I chose a batik I had cut for an area of the harbor at the far left of the quilt. The batik had a brown chevron pattern on a variegated tan to blue background. I selected the blue areas of the fabric for the harbor water because it reminded me of rockweed or kelp floating on the surface of the sea. The lighter tan background of this fabric related to the beige, brown, and blue plaid I had already used in the schooner frame, so I cut into the tan part of the batik for the left of the frame in the harbor area.

This chevron-patterned batik fabric would have been too dark above the point of land on the left side of the schooner frame, and too different from the light sky on either side of it. To make the fabric paler—that is, closer in value to the two sky fabrics—I layered a piece of pale organza over it, simply cutting the batik and the organza, and then piecing both as though they were a single fabric.

I cut the top border of the schooner frame from a beige background print with tiny white and gray vines. This fabric was of a suitable scale and color to go with the other fabrics, or was at least better than anything else I could find. To give the print a slightly stronger presence, I enhanced the vines with a touch of black ink to darken the overall value of the original fabric. The little vines reminded me of several small ground-cover plants that grow in the area.

COLOR, PATTERN, AND SCALE

To add a little color and repeat a little fine-scale geometry, I added a narrow inner border to the schooner frame, above the headlands, and inside the top left frame. I used a beige, white, blue, and red woven stripe for this border; the scale, pattern, and colors of the stripe picked up the small plaids used in the tiny buildings around the harbor.

To depict some of the small buildings ringing the harbor, I took advantage of the geometry of small-scale plaids and stripes. The woven patterns suggested architectural detail such as doors, windows, siding, and trim and gave me an opportunity to add little bits of color to this area of the design. I placed a drying rack—partially pieced with a narrow stripe and partially stitched by machine—next to the large red warehouse in the lower left area of the scene.

Because I chose several fabrics with hints of lavender for the water outside the schooner frame, I chose a lovely hand-dyed fabric to create a lavender sunrise in the upper left area of the quilt. Water reflects the color of the sky in nature, and this combination worked very well to replicate this in the quilt.

I tucked a white building into the lower left corner of the composition, behind the rocky shore which extends toward the right, and then lined the shore with brush-wood flakes. At some seasons of the year, these flakes would have been covered by hundreds of split and salted cod, drying in the open air.

The Border

The quilt top for *The Schooner Change* was finished with a blue plaid border at the top and along part of the right edge. I determined that a single wide strip of blue plaid spanning the top would have been too much, so I inserted a strip of pinkish-lavender-blue upholstery fabric into part of the border for balance. If you cover this strip over, you will see how necessary it is to the composition.

I decided that to use blue plaid all the way down the right side of the quilt would be too much as well, so I added a piece of fabric from the water below the schooner frame to the top of the right border. It related in color and value to the blue plaid, but lacked the strong whites and geometry of the plaid, which would have focused too much attention on the top right corner. The right border was interrupted by the landscape as well.

The blue plaid border disappeared behind the hills on the left edge of the quilt, and then reappeared at the lower left, transformed into a gray calico print among the rocks.

USING TRADITIONAL QUILT BLOCKS

I completed the borders with corner blocks in reference to traditional border style. I used nine-patches, choosing fabrics and colors that worked with the rest of the composition. The corner blocks in the drawing were not perfect squares, so I adjusted the components of each nine-patch to fit the available space.

A narrow outer band of a single gray fabric with greenish triangles completed and set off the design. The quilt felt cramped without this narrow band between the wider border and the binding.

The Quilting

The Schooner Change was free-motion machine quilted with cotton thread, using a variety of patterns to detail the different elements. I used quilting to draw in a few lines of rigging and masts in the distance. Some of the ideas for a quilting pattern came from the subject—the billows of the sails or the waves in the water. Sometimes I used patterns I've used before—the fans in the sky—which may suggest clouds. In other places I drew in details—rigging of the schooner or windows on the houses. On the plaid border below the schooner, I used a sideways chevron pattern suggested by the chevrons on the batik fabric.

The four fishermen in the schooner were hand appliquéd, exploiting the light and dark areas in a print to suggest faces and clothing.

■　■　■　■　■

As I look at this quilt, I think about the boat builders building a boat out of what they had at hand or what they could get. I think about building a house the same way, and building quilts from found fabrics—the challenges of running out of what you thought you needed, and adapting something else in its place. Not easy, but the process is much the same.

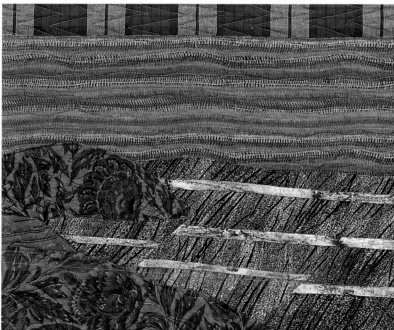

FOUR COMPANIONS

Four Companions, 81" x 69½", © 2002 Ruth B. McDowell

I have read and reread JRR Tolkien's *Lord of the Rings* books many times since I first discovered them in 1963. In addition to the characters and the plot, the imagination displayed in the visual descriptions and the immense depth of detail make these books unique.

Every time I read them, I notice something different. Each society in Middle Earth has a complexity of history, language, and character that is intertwined with the destinies of the characters and threads of the stories.

The relationships that develop between the Tolkien characters, their gradual understanding and acceptance of each other, and the strong bonds that they form on their perilous journey are the backbone of *The Lord of the Rings* books. I greatly admire Peter Jackson's interpretation of the books in film—a daunting task considering such different media and such beloved source material.

Four Companions is my version of the four hobbits, related to Jackson's hobbits only in that both are determined by the very specific descriptions in the Tolkien books.

The Quilt Design

The design of the quilt began when I had a few days off during an out-of-town teaching trip. To amuse myself in an out-of-the-way place, I spent some time making pencil drawings of Frodo, Samwise, Merry, and Pippin. The drawings surprised me by turning out rather well. Each of the four hobbits had a distinct personality.

In my previous quilts, I had avoided piecing facial features. The hard edges of the seams between the pieces made most pieced faces appear masklike. Instead, I'd usually just suggest faces rather than drawing in the details. See *Sliding Goddess with Heart* (page 14) for an example.

DESIGNING FACES
During the remaining time on this trip, I played around with my freehand drawings to see if I could convert them into piecing diagrams. I chose to use straight seams, rather than curves, for their more abstract quality and for the more energetic and dynamic look they typically produce. (Curved seams might have made the hobbits look like cartoon characters.) Amazingly enough, even the straight-seam pieced faces on my hobbits worked well, maintaining the personalities I saw in the drawings.

In translating the drawings of the faces into straight-seam sections for piecing, I tried to follow the planes and folds of the facial features and, at the same time, plan pieces that could be sewn in sequence into sections. Some of the pieces were *very* small.

PLANNING THE PIECING
Very slight shifts in the angle or direction of the seam-lines made subtle but significant differences in the overall look. It was a juggling act to maintain the character I saw in my hobbit drawings and—at the same time—devise a piecing plan I could sew. When I had completed the piecing drawing for each hobbit, I set up the overall composition, tweaking the piecing if necessary to make the group of four fit together.

Once I placed the straight-seam versions of the hobbits on a single large piece of paper, I used the major seamlines to break up the background. I wanted to *suggest* a landscape without making it location-specific and I wanted the relationships between the hobbits to remain the focus of the quilt, supported—but not over-whelmed—by the background.

Because of the many trees in the Tolkien books (in addition to the wonderful ents), I wanted a tree in the quilt, acting almost as an additional character. The tree was deliberately placed near Frodo and was suggested very simply by a few large pieces of elegantly hand-dyed fabrics. I added tumbled rocks, which may (or may not) be stonework from ancient buildings.

THOUGHTS ON PIECING FACES

I continue to go back and forth about the best way to deal with faces in pieced quilts. In some ways, I prefer the undetailed style I've used for faces in some of my other quilts. In *this* quilt, I wanted to try the process of pieced faces, and I think it worked out well for the hobbits.

The challenge to create natural faces might have been far more difficult for the human characters in Tolkien's books. Human faces are so familiar to us that the slight "jar" inherent in straight-seam piecing might become more of an issue. It is likely that pieced human faces would seem too masklike. Hobbits, existing only in the imagination, offer a bit more latitude.

The Fabric

The fabrics in the clothing followed Tolkien's descriptions to some degree. I used woven patterns in the shirts and pants, rather than floral or other prints, recognizing that printed designs would be much more ethnic- and era-specific, while woven patterns could suggest almost any place or time. To make the changeable elfin cloaks, I collected a variety of greenish and grayish fabrics.

THE HOBBITS

Hobbit feet are described as large and furry. This pre-sented a quandary: If I made them *too* furry, I'd loose their shape, especially piecing them at this scale. As a compromise, I used a fabric printed with a feathery pattern to suggest fur on the large, carefully drawn bare feet.

In the beginning of Tolkien's books, hobbits are described as lovers of food and drink, and peaceful inhabitants in the pleasant land of the Shire. Sam, Frodo's gardener, was the cook on the expedition, and an important, though perhaps unexpected, support to his master. Sam kept a remnant of the memory of the Shire alive for Frodo as the horrors of the journey increased.

The hobbit faces were extraordinarily difficult to do. In addition to the technical problems of sewing many tiny interlocking pieces on the sewing machine, I found I needed subtly different values of a very narrow range of skin colors to show the modeling of the faces, without making them appear masklike. The hobbit eyes were cut from a white-background-with-brown-dots vintage fabric a student shared with me a few years ago. (Bless her!) Trying to accomplish this with commercially produced rather than hand-painted fabrics was an exasperating exercise. My daughter says the language coming from the sewing room was not to be believed! Needless to say, I don't plan to do pieced faces again soon.

MAKING A FIRE

I came across a small piece of hand-dyed fabric that had been in my stash for at least fifteen years. It was an unusual combination of colors that shaded from yellowish-red to grayish-brown, and I'd always been puzzled about what to do with it. This fabric made the flames of a perfect little campfire among the rocks, although I had to be very careful when cutting to make sure I had enough.

The cooking pots Sam carried are mentioned several times in the books. It wasn't until I finished the quilt and saw Jackson's film *The Fellowship of the Ring* yet again that I realized my fabric pot looked exactly like the one in the movie. Coincidence, maybe—or perhaps a visual memory I was not aware of at the time.

The Border

I felt the composition could use a little bit of a frame in the top half of the quilt. I had a wonderful big leafy print that worked well with the other fabric choices I had made. As a narrow inner line, I chose small squares of a reddish fabric and a print with some bright light in it. The reds picked up the other uses of red, primarily in the hobbits themselves. The geometry and regular repeat of the squares was created as a counterpoint to the more organic shapes in the rest of the quilt.

The Quilting

I stitched quilting lines as though I were using a pencil on the Hobbit faces and hands, adding creases and folds, fingers and knuckles. I then stitched a curly pattern on their hair, folds and details of their clothing, and fur on their legs and feet. With black thread, I stitched irregular lines on the rocks, changing the angles to make different facets. Ferns and little mosses were stitched between the rocks with variegated green threads. Bark lines on the tree unite the hand-dyes I used and give the tree its own texture. I flattened the background with an overall angular pattern, then drew veins in the large leaves printed in the outer border.

I want my quilts to remain quite unapologetically *quilts,* and not to resemble paintings or photographs. The use of commercial fabrics and my insistence on sticking to traditional piecing methods are both necessary and important in achieving that goal, and are some of the characteristics that give my quilts their very distinctive style.

Each quilt I make is an exploration and an experiment. Sometimes the experiment is fairly straightforward. Sometimes I'm charting really new territory for myself, but then, skating on thin creative and technical ice is the only way to learn what works and what doesn't. *Four Companions* gave me a chance to try something new, and to make a quilt about a book I've loved for years.

I really enjoyed working within and against the limits of the traditional piecing format. It was great fun to combine the piecing technique and commercial fabric to make my version of Middle Earth.

MADAME BLU'S CHICKENS

Madame Blu's Chickens, 29" x 34", © 2003 Ruth B. McDowell

While lecturing in a design class at Madame Blu's quilt store near Copenhagen, Denmark, I was often accompanied by these vociferous black chickens. Apparently, a fox had taken most of the hens, and the remaining roosters were left to compete in a crowing contest.

The chickens were glossy black with bright red combs, and strutted around in the gravel and under the green plants of the chicken yard, looking for food and eyeing me suspiciously. They were very funny and absolutely gorgeous, and eventually demanded a quilt of their own.

The Quilt Design

I worked on the design for this quilt from a photograph I had taken of my noisy companions. If I viewed the image simply as an abstract composition, I liked the placement of the black masses of chicken shapes with the scattering of bright green and red details. As a quilt depicting literal chickens, I liked the look of the big chicken walking off the bottom edge of the quilt, and the one exiting at the upper right.

I settled on a rather small size for the quilt to keep the chickens approximately in scale. (A giant chicken is a scary thought!) I chose a piecing strategy that allowed me to work with ruler-straight seams. This simplified the sewing of the small pieces and maintained the slightly abstract quality I was looking for.

DEVELOPING THE LAYERS

In planning the design drawing, I began with the foremost chicken, allowing the seamlines from this bird to begin dividing the quilt into sewable sections. Next I drew the chicken on the left, allowing its seamlines to break up more of the surface. In the spaces remaining, I added the third bird, the green leaves, and finally the last two chickens in the spaces created by the previous seams.

Working from the foreground of the design to the back in this way caused the chickens in the background to become progressively more fractured. I also included less and less detail in the birds farther back. This progressive simplification enhanced the sense of depth in the picture. I completed the composition by adding some seamlines parallel to the outside edges, both to frame the piece, and to allow me a place to use some stronger fabrics to advance the foreground.

The Fabric

I headed to my stash and pulled a variety of "chicken" fabrics. I found black fabrics with various kinds of patterns to differentiate the various areas of feathers, and very dark blue fabrics to add a little color. I selected and cut the fabric pieces for the large chicken first, and then worked on the three in the group on the left.

In the foremost of these three chickens, I used eight or nine different black prints to differentiate the various groups and types of feathers. I chose a single bluish-black fabric for the bird immediately behind the front chicken to separate the two visually, and then added a few more patterned black fabrics for the bird hiding behind the leaves. The trick was to make all the birds "black" but still let the eye read them as separate animals, while creating an interesting mix of color and pattern in the composition.

THOUGHTS ON PIECING AND FABRIC SELECTION

In making the fabric choices for a pieced image of this kind, you must remain constantly aware of how the result reads visually, and not rely on what you intellectually intended when you chose a particular fabric.

This quilt top is made of pieces of fabric—chickens, leaves, and backgrounds—seamed together. Each piece of fabric in one chicken must hold together visually, and at the same time must contribute to delineating one chicken from another. The quilt is a representation of space, and viewers must be able to understand visually what is "in front" and what is "behind." There aren't any physical clues to spatial relationships as there might be in appliqué, where one fabric can be overlapped on top of another.

TAKING ADVANTAGE OF FABRIC DESIGN

While I did draw some small pieces in the piecing plan to make the combs, I wanted to find a fabric—not solid red—that would let me shade the combs and add additional detail in a scale that would be too small to piece. I found what I needed in a dramatic large-scale print of red poppies on a dark background—a fabric that had been sitting for some time on my fabric shelf. I hadn't bought this fabric to make chickens. It wasn't a fabric I could run out and find in a store when I needed it. It *was* an unusual design with some irregular, high-contrast edges that looked like they might prove useful for something. I rather doubt I'll ever use it for poppies as the designer intended.

Some of the poppies in the print were paler, which worked well for the areas around the chicken eyes. I drew in the eyes with archival black ink, and then added a single white French knot to highlight each eye after the quilting was done. I used several finely patterned brownish fabrics to suggest the ground and gravel, and some small-scale green prints to suggest the weeds in the chicken yard.

The Border

After cutting out some bright green leaves for the upper left area of the quilt, I found a batik with a dark background and light leaves in almost the same shape and size as the green ones I had pieced. I used the batik in the border on the left and top edges of the quilt, carefully cutting the fabric to get just the right part of the print.

In the end, I loved the way my eye traveled back and forth between the pieced leaves and the printed ones in the batik. The pale yellow of the printed leaves was a much better choice for the overall color composition than green printed leaves would have been.

Since a great many of the fabrics I chose for this quilt were busy, small-scale patterns, I selected some larger-scale, bold geometric designs for the border areas at the right edge and at the bottom of the quilt. The red, yellow, and black large-scale African print pulled the bottom edge forward and picked up the reds of the combs, the yellows of the beaks, and the blacks of the chickens.

The Quilting

Madame Blu's Chickens was free-motion quilted with black thread. I used the quilting lines to loosely sketch curved feather details on the birds, extending the lines past the pieced edges and avoiding in-the-ditch stitching. I also drew in the veins of the leaves, again extending past the pieced edges to loosen the design. This looser approach to quilting enlivened the entire quilt and gave it a feeling of motion.

I wanted to stitch hexagonal "chicken wire" as the quilting pattern for most of the background, but knew I would have to draw a grid with chalk or pencil to guide me. Since the fabrics on the front of the quilt were so highly patterned, I turned the quilt over and pencilled a grid on the backing fabric. I could see the outlines of the chickens and leaves on the back of the quilt because I had already quilted them from the front. Guided by the pencilled grid on the back of the quilt, and working from the back, I stitched the chicken-wire pattern in black thread, and filled all areas I had not quilted previously.

The fabrics I used in the quilt top were so highly patterned, that the chicken-wire quilting barely showed from the front—but then, I like hidden surprises. The density of the "chicken wire" was enough to hold the quilt layers together and keeps the top from pillowing out when the quilt has been hanging for a while.

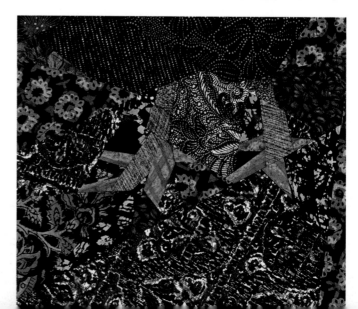

HIMALAYAN BLUE POPPIES

Himalayan Blue Poppies, 52" x 70½", © 2003 Ruth B. McDowell

Meconopsis betonicifolia grows at about 3500 meters in its native southeastern Tibet. I've always been attracted to the downward-facing poppy-like bloom with its crinkled texture and luminous blue color, but it is— alas—a somewhat difficult garden perennial.

I have had a garden for years, and love the idea of its variety of shapes, colors, and textures, but the quilts and the teaching and the writing have made the garden impossible to maintain. The sturdier plants remain, but in a rather *au naturel* style. Fussy plants like this wonderful *Meconopsis* are beyond me.

The Quilt Design

I made drawings using photographs of the poppy taken from several angles with its buds, stems, and leaves, and another of a flower that had almost gone by. I organized my drawings into a composition that pleased me. I chose to maintain, in the piecing drawing, the crinkled texture of the petals, and the pale green and yellow stamens and pistils in the center of the flowers. This required reducing these small parts to simple shapes, and finding patterns in fabrics to suggest the details. (In other quilts, I have added these details with quilting stitches or embroidery.)

The seamlines in the drawing were a combination of slightly curved, angled, and straight lines. I deliberately tried to give the curved seams some character, with irregularities rather than smooth, swooping curves. I felt this better described the shape of the living poppy, but these irregularities did make these seams somewhat trickier to sew.

Some of the seamlines were extended to simplify the sections for sewing, and to carry the shape of the poppies across the whole composition.

I decided to compose the quilt in a vertical rectangle, choosing a size and shape to fit with the plants I had drawn. To visually strengthen the outer edges of the composition, I drew in the suggestion of a pieced border with a few ruler-straight seamlines that paralleled the edges of the rectangle, but were broken by the seaming that defined the plant.

The Fabric

The *Meconopsis* flower is composed of four petals— a structural detail I wanted to emphasize in the quilt design. I began planning the color of the quilt by pulling some lavender-blue fabrics for the flowers and some medium greens for the stems and leaves from my stash. I found I had to go fabric shopping (!) to get enough periwinkle blues, which are, for some reason, much harder to find than other shades of blue.

I planned the buds to be slightly brighter, lighter, yellower greens. I chose a pale stripe to make the stems of the stamens, a yellow calico (used both right and wrong side up) for the pollen, and a pale-green drapery fabric—wrong side up to make it even lighter—for the stigmas.

BLOCKS OF COLOR

I liked the four shafts of light fabrics radiating from the flower on the left, but wanted to subdue the crosslike imagery to avoid any implication that this was a "Christian" quilt. This was to be a quilt about a poppy, not a religious statement. Some simple geometric shapes have acquired connotations over time that make them difficult to use without introducing unwanted symbolism.

I decided to use the seaming I had already drawn to break the background into large areas of color. The dark golds in the background pieces in the upper left and the lower right minimized to some degree the starkness of the cross shape, while allowing me to keep the four light rays. Three other sections of the background were cut from medium-dark brick-red fabrics, and the remaining upper right section from dark blues and greens.

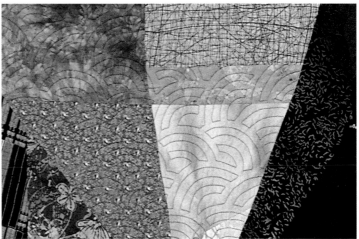

BACKGROUND FABRICS

Having made these fabric selections to create my vision of the poppies, I began to consider fabric and color choices for the rest of the background pieces of the quilt. In my stash, I found several dark fabrics for background, each with a printed or woven pattern, and each containing either some light or some blues, greens, or other touches of color.

I decided to center a lighter, four-armed cross on the flower on the left of the composition to reinforce the geometry of four-petaled *Menocopsis*. To make this cross, I chose some very pale yellow and white fabrics for four of the narrow background areas radiating from the flower. After cutting these lighter pieces of fabric, I began selecting darker fabrics for the background pieces in the lower left quadrant of the quilt.

A two-week teaching trip interrupted the process. When I got back to the quilt, I quickly realized that continuing with the dark background fabrics across the entire quilt was a boring idea, and would make the light cross too prominent in the composition.

MULTICOLOR FABRICS

It was tricky to choose fabrics for these background areas to complement the lighter blues and greens I'd chosen for the plant, to make a composition that balanced visually, and at the same time to make the background support—but not overwhelm—the poppy plant. The brick reds needed enough color without too much intensity, and could not be too orange or too purple. Each fabric also needed a different kind of pattern, as the exact placement and mix of each pattern would play a significant part in the overall design of the quilt.

Many of the background fabrics had touches of other colors, which helped unify the surface and make all the fabrics work together. Most of the background fabrics were used more than once, which helped move the eye around the quilt.

This is really the first time I can remember incorporating large blocks of color in the background of a plant quilt. The size of this quilt, and the number and scale of plant elements in the overall design, may have helped to make the complex background successful. I suspect it would have been much more difficult to balance on a smaller quilt, or with a simpler drawing.

The Border

It's all a matter of perspective as to whether or not this quilt has a border. Because of the color-block construction, if there is a border, it consists of a few seams parallel to the outside edges of the quilt. Only on the lower left, did I make color changes in these outside strips, to pull some reds to the left side and balance their placement in the rest of the quilt.

The Quilting

I used cotton threads—variegated on the flowers and leaves, and black on the background—for the free-motion quilting. On the various parts of the plant, I drew in the veining and other details, matching the colors of the threads to the flower or leaf. An overall fan pattern in the background united the various fabrics, flattened the surface, and put the plant into relief. With such an elaborate background color scheme, it was important to find a pattern, such as the overall fan pattern, to serve as a unifying factor.

■ ■ ■ ■ ■

The plant in *Himalayan Blue Poppies* feels very crisp and clean, almost as if beaded with early-morning dew. The quilt illustrates and celebrates this wonderful plant in the way I intended, and I'm very pleased with the color and the overall composition. The experiment with the color-block background was certainly a success, and an idea that I'll use again.

OSEBERG SHIP

T he beautiful spirals at the stem and stern of the Oseberg ship have stuck in
my mind since I first saw pictures of them years ago. Surely the tight curls of fiddle-
head ferns in early spring inspired these spirals. This 1000-year-old ship was found in

The Oseberg ship was apparently a pleasure barge for a river or sheltered bay. It carried a mast and square sail, but could also be rowed. Viking ships were sometimes described as Serpents of the Sea; indeed, the hulls flex to conform to the sea surface. Notice the difference at the center of the two large spirals: the bow spiral (at the left) ends in a "head" and the stern spiral (at the right) with a pointed "tail."

The Quilt Design

In making the drawings for this quilt, I wanted to include details of the two spirals, as well as several views of the entire ship. To accomplish this, I decided to treat them all as elements in an abstract composition. Rather than putting the Oseberg ship in the water, I decided to suspend it over an oval pool of blue.

PIECING CONSIDERATIONS

I liked the concept of making the construction seams part of the design. If you look carefully at the white area in the center of the quilt, you will see a gentle horizontal curve that is basically a construction seam for the top end of the masts. I used this seam to change the fabrics in

the background. Study the composition further and you will find many more construction seams. Basically, I needed these seams to sew various parts of the quilt, but I also used them as opportunities to add many additional fabrics to the quilt. In drawing each of these seams, I was careful to make the seamline an attractive part of the overall composition.

I started a long, curved, vertical seam at the top of the quilt, on the right side of the gold fabric. I continued this seam almost all the way to the bottom of the design, bisecting the large open boat. As a construction seam, this was one of the last seams I sewed, joining the two halves of the pieced top together. I used this seam to shift some of the fabrics in the pool of blue at the bottom of the image.

USING CONSTRUCTION SEAMS AS DESIGN ELEMENTS

It didn't bother me that this seam took a graceful path through the middle of the boat. I placed the seam there because of my piecing process. The seam is less prominent in the bisected boat because I used similar fabrics on both sides of the seam. Above and below the boat, I deliberately used the seamline to shift the fabrics on both sides. As in many of my quilts, this interplay of the construction process and the abstract composition gave my pieced quilt structural integrity as well as contributing to the overall design.

In addition to the necessary construction seams, I added some curved seams in the background in the upper part of the quilt. These seams echoed and expanded upon the various spirals and, once again, allowed me to add more fabrics, so the additional seams and fabrics became parts of the overall composition.

The Fabric

I wanted high value contrast in the fabrics for *Oseberg Ship*. I found a variety of very light fabrics for the majority of the background, and some very dark browns for the ships. The ship fabrics in the enlarged details of the bow and stern were more patterned and were slightly lighter browns than the hand-dyed browns on the two views of the ship. The actual ship had a great deal of carving on the bow and stern, and the patterned fabrics were intended to imply this detail.

In the background, I used an African print and a black and white Marimekko print; both contained geometric elements I thought suggested traditional Viking designs. In the top center of the background I used a large piece of a slipcover fabric—a heavier, cotton twill fabric printed with a sort of patchwork design in whites and grays. This fabric also contained a few little printed spirals, repeating the spirals on the boats. A batik with large circles, divided between white and black and repeating the circular shapes of the boat spirals, added a strong pattern to the upper right of the composition and a

spot of light in the lower part of the pool of blue water. I wanted to encourage eye movement around the quilt, and I often find repeating a specific fabric in different places and in different ways an effective way to do this. I also wanted to play with the geometry of the boat in the selection of the other fabrics in the quilt.

FORT MORRISON JERSEYS

Since I was a little girl, my family has owned an old summer place in the hills of Colrain in western Massachusetts. We always anticipated the end of the long trip to "The Farm" as we drove through the valley of the North River past Fort Morrison Farm. The fields were full of chicken coops, and hundreds of red-brown chickens running here and there—a very exciting sight to small children. The place was on the site of old Fort Morrison, built as protection for the families in the

The fields at Fort Morrison Farm are now home to a beautiful herd of Jersey cows, whose milk is used to make Cabot's cheeses. I remember being amazed at Jerseys as I looked though the *Jersey Journal* at Sara Dillow's kitchen table in Nebraska. In addition to the classic golden-fawn color I had seen most often, I discovered that Jerseys vary in color from a very pale cream to an almost charcoal brown.

As I drove past one summer, the herd at Fort Morrison was waiting outside the barn in the golden sunlight of late afternoon. The cows were a parade of every possible Jersey color, and quite a sight to see with the green fields and the bright blue sky as a backdrop. I returned to the farm with my camera a few weeks later, and was kindly given permission to take some photographs. A row of young cattle poked their heads out through the bars of a shed. The heads were in bright sunlight, while the shed itself cast a deep shadow across the their backs. At the far side of the shed, the shadow was broken by glimpses of the sky.

The Quilt Design

The repeated images, along with the great individuality of these five young cattle, and the terrific play of light, shadows, and colors led—of course—to another quilt. The image here is taken very literally from one of my photographs. (It was a good photograph!) The architecture of the shed framed the image beautifully, with strong verticals and diagonals and gleams of light coming through cracks between the boards.

The calf at the right was very interested in what I was doing, while perhaps the other four were looking for a handout.

The complexity of the overlapping calves made planning the piecing rather complicated. I decided to use straight-seam piecing which is visually a little more abstract or quiltlike. I also wanted to use many different fabrics to get the shading on the cattle just right, and recognized that straight-seam piecing was a much more practical way to assemble the many pieces I intended to use.

The Fabric

I tried to keep the shades and colors of the individual calves as I saw them in the photograph. To separate them visually and to individualize their personalities, I collected slightly different fabrics for each. I needed some very slight differences in value, but was able to pull fabrics from my stash in the variety I needed. Using some fabrics both right side up and wrong side up gave me even more subtly different values to work with. A purchased piece of discharge-dyed black fabric with streaks of brown became very useful, especially for the back of the calf at the right.

I used a collection of gray fabrics for the repeating bars of the metal stanchions, placing each fabric in the same position along the row. This strategy strengthened the sense of repetition, and the quilt benefited from the consistency.

USING PLAIDS AND STRIPES

While the rest of the fabrics in the quilt are cotton, the wide horizontal gray bar in the center of the quilt was a linen plaid—a remnant from some dressmaking project. Although I usually stick to cotton fabrics, linen handles almost the same in sewing and doesn't need special care if cleaning is required.

I used an ikat woven-stripe fabric with touches of gold, blue, and green at the bottom right corner of the quilt as the front of the concrete curb. This fabric made a visual connection with colors elsewhere in the quilt. I had to piece the fabric to get large enough pieces, paying attention to the spacing of the black vertical stripe. The stripe echoed the vertical stripes of the gray stanchions and the broad vertical posts of the shed on a smaller scale.

I could see faraway trees in the light open area at the top of the quilt and I used a collection of blue-green fabrics—some wrong side up to get the right value—to suggest the tree-covered hills in an abstract and quiltlike way.

The narrow light streaks between the boards at the back of the shed were a wonderful part of the original photograph, and greatly enhanced the composition of the quilt. The light streaks angled downward, in opposition to the upward angle of the horizontal bars of the stanchions.

The Border

The geometry of the shed provided a good frame for the calves; the size of the overall quilt as I had sewn it was the right scale for the group of cattle. The post on the right and the lights and darks at the top and to the left act as a border in those areas.

The ikat stripe used for the light gray wedge at the lower right, which was poured concrete in the actual shed, also functions as part of the border. A solid light concrete-gray fabric, although more realistic, would not have worked as well in the composition.

The Quilting

I did free-motion quilting with black and variegated golden thread on the cattle to add creases and folds to their skin. To lift the stanchion bars from the background, I quilted in-the-ditch around each one, and then used a series of almost straight quilting lines to flatten areas of the background. I quilted the light open area at the top of the shed in an overall pattern of fan quilting, perhaps suggesting the shapes of the treetops I could see in the photograph.

■ ■ ■ ■ ■

This quilt had more little pieces than I often use, and was therefore a bit paint-by-numberish. I go back and forth in the process of quiltmaking—sometimes I will leave out detail and try to create the image I want with simpler, larger shapes, letting the pattern of the fabrics do more of the design work. Sometimes I get involved in the details and in making lots of subtle value changes with many pieces of fabric.

In this case, the little pieces were necessary to differentiate the parts of each calf and to separate the overlapping images of the five animals. In contrast to this detailed piecing, I used bigger pieces in a more abstract manner in the rest of the quilt. That shift in piecing keeps the focus where it belongs: on the wonderful group of golden Jerseys.

SAWTOOTH TULIP

Sawtooth Tulip, 53" x 35", © 2004 Ruth B. McDowell

I love looking at the details in natural forms. The centers of many flowers contain striking colors, patterns, and shapes. The stamens and pistils are like tiny sculptures framed by the bright colors of the petals.

Tulips often have especially dramatic centers. In many parrot tulips, those centers are set off by the swirling patterns of their opulent flaring, streaked, and fringed petals. They are some of my favorites. Some years ago I made a quilt with a pair of red and yellow tulips, using a more naturalistic style of curved and inset-corner seams. I set the tulips in a larger space and contrasted them with several smaller, simpler tulip blocks, and other geometric elements. The quilt is called *Parrot Tulips* and appears in *Art & Inspirations: Ruth B. McDowell* (C&T Publishing, 1996, out of print).

The Quilt Design

Recently I decided to revisit the tulips, but to tighten the focus on the center of one flower, and to create a more abstract image with straight seams. In making the drawing from which I pieced this quilt, I cropped the image so the tulip occupies almost the whole quilt surface, keeping just enough of the ragged tulip edges to suggest the whole, and to allow for a bit of a contrasting color in the background.

It can be tricky to take such a curvilinear flower and reduce it to a series of straight lines, while still keeping the feel of the original. To get the effect I wanted, it was critical not to include too much detail. I think the pattern of seams I designed for this quilt was just about right.

PIECING CONSIDERATIONS

If you hunt for them, you may be able to find the long, straight seams that divide this image into a network of straight-sided sections. The section lines are hidden to some degree because the areas of red and areas of yellow cross them in irregular ways. If the edge of one

section were red and the next only yellow, these seams would stand out dramatically. I also incorporated straight seams within the sections, which were designed to be pieced, in a logical order. I love working within the limits of piecing to produce the images I have in mind.

While engineering was a part of the decision-making process here, it was not—by any means—just engineering. I needed an overall piecing plan that would make an interesting graphic composition, with a variety of piece sizes and a mix of angles that would work together visually as a composition. I avoided any seams that ran parallel to the outside edges of the quilt; the viewer's eye would have picked up the horizontal and vertical seams very quickly. As a result, these straight lines would have broken the sweep of the slanting diagonal seams, and blocked the movement I was after.

The selection of straight seams on a flower of this shape produced many small triangular pieces of bright color in the design. This reminded me of many traditional quilts with small bright sawtooth elements. I liked this historical parallel and it influenced my selection for the title of this piece.

The Fabric

Within an actual tulip petal, the red and yellow colors blend in complex streaky patterns that are impossible to find in commercial fabrics, or—at least—in the fabrics that existed in my stash. This forced me to abstraction, and required a pattern drawn with distinct areas of red fabric pieces and yellow fabric pieces to suggest the impression of tulip colors and to work graphically in the composition. I found the process of working within the limits of the available fabric much more interesting than taking up a brush and painting red and yellow tulip-petal fabric.

VALUE AND INTENSITY

I needed to balance the range of values and intensities of the red and yellow fabrics, as well as the variety of printed or woven patterns, both in working out the interpretation of the tulip and in developing the overall composition. As I made more decisions, the process of decision-making began to shift from the original tulip image to the completion of the developing quilt.

I selected the fabrics for the pistil and stamens at the center of the tulip from both points of view as well. I wanted the stamens to appear black and different in texture, with reflections and light and shadow increasing their complexity. I used several different dark prints, most with touches of colors other than black. The pistil was composed of two fabrics, smoother in texture than the stamens, and pale green in color.

BACKGROUND FABRICS

For the small areas of the background, I chose a variety of medium greens with a slightly blue cast. The greens here reinforced the green in the pistil. Several background fabrics had black prints, which referred the eye to the small black details in the stamens at the center. The exact placement of each green background fabric was carefully determined to work with and complete the overall composition.

The Border

This quilt was complete without a border. The tight crop of the flower filled the image, and the amount of background was proportionate to the image. The addition of a border would have stopped the flow of the diagonal motion. The design worked well as a graphic image, whether or not the tulip was even recognized.

The Quilting

I free-motion machine quilted this quilt using variegated cotton threads: red for the tulip and green for the background. A pattern of curves, suggesting the shape of the actual tulip petals, was stitched across the tulip. Tight black meander quilting added texture to the stamens, while the green backgrounds in the outer edges were quilted with a fan design, reminiscent of traditional hand quilting.

The curves in the quilting designs complemented the straight seaming in this quilt. All of the quilting was done freehand, with no marked designs. It is all shifted slightly away from the actual pieced seams.

■ ■ ■ ■ ■

Sawtooth Tulip has perhaps a narrower range of fabrics and colors than some of my other art quilts. It is essentially red, yellow, and blueish green, with touches of black. The colors are all very clear. With the exception of the stamens, most of the fabrics are light or medium values; however, within that narrower range of fabrics, there were subtle distinctions in type of print and scale of pattern to consider. I think the overall fabric selection makes for a very happy quilt, with a lot of motion in it, and one that offers a bright reminder of spring.

MOOSEWOOD

Moosewood, or *Acer pensylvanicum*, is a small, wide-spreading understory tree or shrub native to the woodlands of northeastern North America. It is the only native American member of the Snake-Bark maples, with the others being native to China and Japan. The small trunks are

The older trunks are covered with a very smooth bark of an intricately beautiful, but subtler pattern of gray, green, and white. Moosewood is very, very slow growing; a really large one might be 5" or 6" in diameter. The name Moosewood probably comes from the fact that it is good winter browse for moose.

Moosewood leaves are bright green, turning butter yellow in the fall. The winged seed pairs (or *samaras*) are a classic maple shape. The very small, pretty flowers hang in short strings. While I love this tree, and have shifted a few small ones to my yard where they seem quite happy, moosewood is usually not recommended for suburban landscapes.

The Quilt Design

While most people identify trees by their differing leaf shapes, each tree species has many other unique characteristics. The branching pattern, flowers, seeds, bark, and wood are unique in different trees. This maple, like many others, spaces its leaves to catch the most light; the leaves are angled in mostly horizontal layers, so none shade the others.

The leaf pattern I observed became the starting point for the drawing for this quilt. I *very* slightly shifted a few leaves and pruned a few away, but kept the branching structure. Next, I changed the orientation and cropped the image to get the drawing of leaves I wanted. Then I drew in the suggestion of a trunk and branches behind the leaves, although they're certainly not to scale.

ARTISTIC LICENSE

Anyone growing up in maple country has a fondness for the pairs of winged seeds, which spin like helicopters as they fall. I took some artistic license by including the seeds with fall foliage; they do not coincide in nature. In placing the seeds in a row at the upper left of the composition, I recalled the placement of calligraphy in Oriental paintings. I curved and turned the seeds slightly so the vertical row would imply the motion of their fall. The seed near the bottom left corner of the quilt balanced the composition nicely.

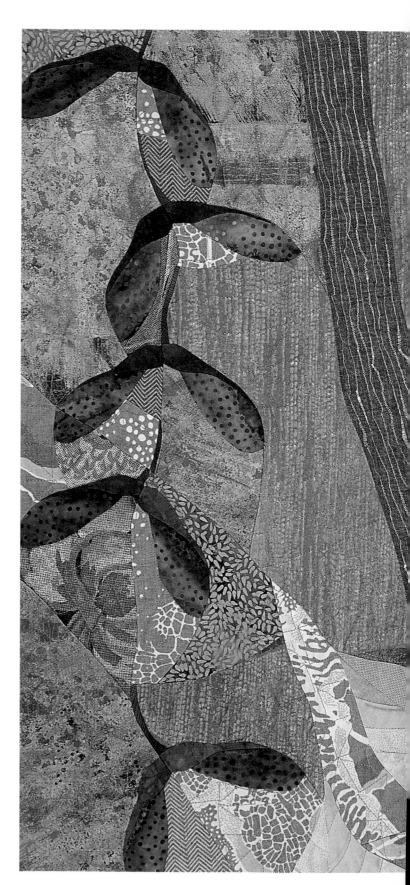

Gently curved seams followed the veining pattern of the leaves and the shape of the trunk and seeds. In some cases, I placed different fabrics between the vein seams. In other cases, I made a section of leaf from a single piece of fabric, and added the veins with machine quilting.

The Fabric

I chose to make the leaves slightly paler yellow than they appear in nature, and included some green ones as well, because I wanted to work with those colors. The small stems were not solid brown, but a large-scale ombre plaid with red and blue. The colors of the actual twigs are amazingly varied when you look at them closely.

The actual seeds are not as red as I chose to make them; my choice was a decision based on composition. I slightly decreased the value and intensity of the reds in the seeds from the top to the bottom of the column, placing a stronger, purpler red in the last seed in the lower left corner. This was a subtle touch many may not notice, but which I think is terrific.

GRAY FABRICS

I wanted this to be a quilt soft in color, and had four or five pieces of circa-1985 gray decorator or furnishing fabrics in my stash. None of these fabrics were gray because they were made from white fabric colored with black dye. Each was a mixture of several colors that appeared gray when viewed from a distance. The subtle hues in these fabrics interacted with the yellows, greens, and reds in the other fabrics in the quilt to make a much more interesting color composition than gray made from black dye.

THOUGHTS ON GRAYS

I learned about using grays made from blended colors about 20 years ago from my good friend Rhoda Cohen. Surprisingly, this distinction makes a tremendous difference. Unfortunately the manufacturers of many gray fabrics, especially the ones made for the quilting industry, haven't learned this yet...or perhaps it's just less expensive to make gray fabric with black dye.

Two of the gray fabrics had very large-scale prints. One had bright white dots and lines and netting patterns, and a few areas of brown. The bright white added a sparkle to the surface of the quilt, much like flashes of sunlight, and gave the surface a certain airiness. The other fabric, a chintz, had a very irregular and wide-spaced brush-stroke pattern of darker grays. The brush strokes were about 1^1/$_2$" to 2" wide, and the fabric had hints of blues, pinks, lavenders, and greens.

CREATING SHADOWS

As I began to cut the brushstroke fabric, I realized that, if I were careful, I could cut it so the darker brush-strokes formed shadows under some of the leaves. This put a darker edge under some of the lighter leaves, throwing more emphasis onto the leaves themselves, and separating them from the background. I indicated where I wanted the shadow lines on the back of some of the freezer-paper background templates, and then looked for an area of the fabric pattern to match.

At the top and left of the background I used a piece of slipcover twill, gray in appearance, but actually including many other colors. Toward the center and lower edge of the background, I used a bluish-gray decorator fabric with dime-sized white dots and stems and leaves—a great addition to the other grays and in a different scale and type of pattern.

THOUGHTS ON MULTICOLOR PRINTS

I wish it were easier to find subtle multicolor prints like these, as well as larger-scale designs, more irregular patterns, and more patterns that are abstract (not flowers, leaves, turtles, and frogs). Polka dots that are distributed in a wildly irregular pattern are great in quilts, but most polka dots are evenly spaced so that each piece you cut appears identical to the next.

But, I admit, I'd probably go out of business very quickly if I filled a fabric store with this kind of stuff. It takes some imagination to figure out what to do with it.

The Border

As with *Sawtooth Tulip* (page 90), I felt this design was complete without a border, so I didn't add one—unless you choose to consider the vertical row of seeds on the left a border treatment.

The Quilting

I quilted the leaves using a variegated cotton thread to draw in the veining pattern, and deliberately extended the stitching a little past the edges of the leaves to loosen them up. The background was quilted in gray thread in an overall angular pattern in crisp contrast to the curves in the piecing.

Now and then, I'd mistakenly hit the wrong part of the screen, and need to start again. This is rubbing-your-head-and-patting-your-tummy-and-dancing-on-the-head-of-a-pin stuff: a real challenge for any quilter!

■ ■ ■ ■ ■

I'm very happy with *Moosewood*. In addition to expressing my love of this tree species and working well as a visual composition, it is introducing this great native plant to many people who have never seen it. This is a great bonus from my point of view.

CONCLUSION

I hope you've enjoyed seeing these quilts and learning a little about the process (and the artist) as you've read the text and looked at the photographs.

For the readers who are quiltmakers, I hope the ideas here will be helpful to you when you are making your own quilts.

For the readers who are new to the idea of quilts that are meant to be hung on the wall as art, I hope this book has given you a foundation to see these quilts with the appreciation they deserve.

I love making quilts, especially ones like these that are important to me for so many reasons.

Peace.

When I quilted the trunk, I attempted to interpret the pattern in the moosewood bark. I hadn't been able to find the right kind of printed fabric for the trunk, so I used white cotton thread to zigzag a tight, but not-quite-satin stitch, over the greenish-gray chambray I had chosen, randomly changing the width of the stitch as I went.

The Pfaff sewing machine I currently use has a touch screen. As I tried to juggle the bulk of the quilt and direct the quilting for the zigzag white stripes, I needed to hit the stitch width control of the touch screen in an irregular pattern, all without doing myself bodily harm.

ABOUT THE AUTHOR

Ruth B. McDowell is an internationally known professional quilt artist, teacher, lecturer, and author. She has made over 300 quilts during the last two decades. Her quilts have been seen in many solo shows, as well as in dozens of magazines and books. Ruth resides in Winchester, Massachusetts. Visit Ruth's website at www.ruthbmcdowell.com.

Other Books by Ruth B. McDowell

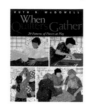  

INDEX